Laura Miller

ENGLISCHE ÜBUNGSGRAMMATIK

Grammatik
— genau und leicht erklärt
— intensiv eingeübt
— für Schule, Nachhilfe und Selbststudium

Band II:
Lösungen zun Übungen von Band I
mit ausführlichem Vokabelverzeichnis

Laura Miller Verlag

2. Auflage — 1991

Copyright Laura Miller Verlag, Köln, 1991

Alle Rechte vorbehalten.

Das Werk, einschließlich aller seiner Teile, ist urheberrechtlich geschützt. Jede Verwertung außerhalb der engen Grenzen des Urheberrechtsgesetzes ist ohne Zustimmung des Verlages unzuläßig und strafbar. Das gilt insbesondere für Vervielfältigungen, Übersetzungen, Mikroverfilmungen und die Einspeicherung und Verarbeitung in elektronischen Systemen.

Druck: Luthe-Druck, Köln

ISBN 3-923954-03-4

Inhalt

1. Personal Pronouns (Personalpronomen) 5
2. Present simple — Present progressive 6
3. Question formation in Present
   (Fragebildung in der Gegenwart) 7
4. Past tense (Vergangenheit) 8
5. Past simple — Past progressive 11
6. Question formation in the Past
   (Fragebildung in der Vergangenheit) 13
7. Question formation (Fragebildung) 15
8. Past — Present Perfect 19
9. Verb tenses (Zeitformen) 20
10. The Comparison of adjectives
    (Die Steigerung der Adjektive) 22
11. If-clauses (Bedingungssätze) 23
12. Question Tags (Angehängte Fragen) 25
13. Relative Clauses (Relativsätze) 26
14. Passive 29
15. Reported Speech (Indirekte Rede) 33
16. Some — any 38
17. Adverbials 39
18. Reflexive Pronouns (das Reflexivpronomen) 41
19. Future (Zukunft) 42
20. Auxiliaries (Modalverben) 43
21. Gerunds (das Gerundium) 49
22. Participles 52
23. The infinitive with and without „to" 54
24. Adverbial clauses 56

Vocabulary (Vokabeln) 59

Personal Pronouns

1. Personal Pronouns

1. They, Their 2. He, He, him, his 3. They, them 4. you 5. Her 6. He, his 7. our, it 8. They, us, them 9. It 10. He, her 11. We, it 12. Her 13. His 14. Our 15. them, They 16. you 17. you 18. us 19. Our, them 20. He, him 21. Her 22. Their, They, them 23. her, She, it 24. his, He, They, them 25. us, Our, We 26. you, I, your, me, me 27. They, Their 28. them, him, her, her, He 29. He 30. her 31. them 32. They 33. him 34. I, my 35. It 36. you, you 37. your 38. She 39. his 40. We 41. our 42. They 43. us 44. his 45. She 46. We 47. They 48. them 49. their 50. your 51. She 52. He 53. it, it 54. him 55. your 56. He 57. your 58. you 59. them 60. you 61. us 62. you 63. It 64. their 65. her 66. it 67. you 68. him 69. our 70. his 71. Her 72. I 73. They 74. She 75. Its 76. We 77. She, it 78. He, him 79. They, them 80. She, it 81. He, it 82. he, it 83. he, them 84. He, her 85. They, it 86. it 87. They, them 88. They, it 89. She, them 90. He, it 91. They, him 92. you 93. you 94. We, them 95. They, them 96. him 97. her 98. She 99. you 100. Its 101. They 102. you 103. Her 104. I 105. We 106. us 107. your 108. It 109. them 110. you 111. it 112. his 113. you 114. our 115. He 116. you 117. us 118. him 119. you 120. her 121. I 122. them 123. you 124. They 125. her 126. you 127. hers 128. They 129. He 130. them 131. theirs 132. it 133. her 134. your 135. your 136. their 137. you 138. it 139. She 140. my 141. It 142. me 143. it 144. it 145. you 146. It 147. They 148. her 149. you 150. He, it 151. them 152. I 153. my 154. you 155. me 156. Her 157. their 158. We 159. him 160. his 161. us

2. Present simple — Present progressive

1. is barking, barks   2. have, is wearing, is wearing   3. go, go   4. leaves, is leaving   5. sits, am sitting   6. get up, are getting up   7. take, are taking   8. speak, are speaking   9. rings, is ringing   10. stop   11. drinks, is drinking   12. doing, is repairing   13. feed, are feeding   14. clean, are cleaning   15. play, plays   16. plays, am playing   17. are going, goes   18. see, are seeing   19. run, are running   20. gets   21. sit   22. is sleeping   23. are making, make   24. take, are taking   25. am speaking, speak   26. play, are playing   27. dance   28. brushes   29. do   30. is flying, flies   31. watches   32. are talking, talk   33. runs, is running   34. is getting up, gets up   35. sit, are sitting   36. Are you sleeping, sleep   37. see, am seeing   38. buy   39. am taking, take   40. brush, brushes   41. makes, are making   42. is flying, flies   43. speak, are speaking   44. are walking, walk, is walking   45. is waiting   46. gets   47. go   48. is pushing   49. is carrying   50. go   51. barks   52. eats   53. are playing   54. watches   55. is coming, are running   56. fly   57. stays   58. goes   59. is putting   60. are speaking   61. eat   62. watches   63. am writing   64. sit   65. swim   66. is riding   67. see   68. carry   69. are flying   70. brush   71. feed   72. is sleeping   73. gets   74. buy   75. is running   76. are taking   77. are writing   78. goes   79. carries   80. run   81. are buying   82. are sitting   83. get up   84. are taking   85. am running   86. watches   87. is putting   88. is carrying   89. play   90. are getting   91. is feeding   92. watch   93. are eating   94. fly   95. rub   96. am shutting   97. flies   98. are leaving   99. is folding   100. swim   101. are sitting   102. are riding   103. do   104. drink   105. does   106. comb   107. are standing   108. spell   109. are smoking   110. brushes   111. is lapping   112. am cutting   113. eat   114. buys   115. are hurting   116. read   117. wash   118. are stretching   119. goes   120. carry   121. are playing, play   122. is ringing, get up   123. walk, are walking   124. is sitting, sits   125. have, are having   126. are waiting   127. has, chews   128. is making   129. takes   130. help   131. drink, are drinking   132. is starting   133. Rub   134. am rubbing   135. draw   136. is feeding, feeds   137. goes, is going   138. leave, is leaving   139. watch, are watching   140. He is coming now. , Now he is coming.   141. The boys often play tennis.   142. He is combing his hair at the moment. , At the moment he is combing his hair.   143. The teacher is already waiting in the classroom.   144. I always forget to eat the slice of bread.

Question formation in the Present

3. Question formation in the Present

1. Who is running home now? 2. Where is the boy running now? 3. When is the boy running home? 4. How is the boy running? 5. Why is the boy running quickly? 6. Is the boy running home now? 7. What is the boy doing now? 8. Who can run home now? 9. When can the boy run home? 10. Who is running home now? 11. Where are two girls running now? 12. How many girls are running home now? 13. When are two girls running home? 14. How are two girls running? 15. Why are two girls running quickly? 16. Are two girls running quickly? 17. What are two girls doing now? 18. Who must run home now? 19. Where must two girls run now? 20. Who is eating an apple now? 21. What am I eating now? 22. When am I eating an apple? 23. How am I eating an apple? 24. Why am I eating an apple quickly? 25. Am I eating an apple? 26. Where am I eating an apple? 27. What am I doing now? 28. Who can eat an apple now? 29. When can I eat an apple? 30. Who runs home every day? 31. Where does the boy run every day? 32. When does the boy run home? 33. How does the boy run? 34. Why does the boy run quickly? 35. Does the boy run quickly? 36. What does the boy do every day? 37. Who can run home every day? 38. When must the boy run home? 39. Who runs home every day? 40. Where do two girls run every day? 41. How many girls run home every day? 42. When do two girls run home? 43. How do two girls run? 44. Why do two girls run quickly? 45. Do two girls run quickly? 46. What do two girls do every day? 47. Who can run quickly? 48. How can two girls run? 49. Who eats an apple every day? 50. What do I eat every day? 51. When do I eat an apple? 52. How do I eat an apple? 53. Why do I eat an apple quickly? 54. Do I eat an apple quickly? 55. What do I do quickly? 56. Who is coming? 57. How many birds are flying? 58. When does the father come home? 59. Where is the boy sitting? 60. What is the girl drinking? 61. What am I writing? 62. Whose mother is here? 63. How is the boy running? 64. Where are the birds? 65. Who is talking? 66. How many children are here? 67. Why is the baby crying? 68. Who eats cake? 69. Where do the men eat? 70. How many dogs bark every day? 71. Can we drive the car? 72. What do you do? 73. When do I see the tree? 74. Where are the girls sleeping? 75. How does the child read? 76. Where are the boys driving? 77. When do I sell books? 78. How are you talking? 79. How many books can the tall man carry? 80. Who writes five books? 81. Are the women coming now? 82. What does the little girl write? 83. Why are you sitting? 84. How many times must the dog bark? 85. Where are you standing? 86. Does he live in a house? 87. What am I wearing? 88. Who often stands in the bus? 89. Who flies a plane? 90. What is the cat eating? 91. Does the little girl read books? 92. Can she read books? 93. Is the girl reading books? 94. Where are we arriving? 95. Do the children talk? 96. Can the children talk? 97. Are the children talking? 98. Do I always walk? 99. Am I walking? 100. Are we holding hands?

4. Past tense

1. My sister usually saw Mr. Smith.   2. The boys were swimming   3. You often left . . .   4. We sometimes took . . .   5. They always wiped . . .   6. My brother rubbed . . .   7. The boy was running . . .   8. Did you often write . . . ?   9. The elephants often lifted . . .   10. My brother always made . . .   11. We were driving . . .   12. The teacher came . . .   13. I was drawing . . .   14. My father had . . .   15. He was writing . . .   16. They always brushed . . .   17. The baby cried . . .   18. I usually fed . . .   19. We always said what we did . . .   20. They often saw . . .   21. You always stepped . . .   22. He was sitting . . .   23. They usually had . . .   24. He danced . . .   25. We always came . . .   26. The boys were laughing . . .   27. The girl always shook her head when she put . . .   28. That boy carried . . .   29. We bought . . .   30. The boys usually played . . .   31. The father held . . .   32. She replied, "You always stuck . . ."   33. Lions always roared when they arrived . . .   34. The child went to the door when it saw that its mother was coming.   35. Did he leave the house when you told . . .   36. The dogs barked because the men were running.   37. I made . . .   38. She got up . . .   39. You ate . . .   40. He cried when he was hurt.   41. Who knew . . .   42. He took . . .   43. We ate . . .   44. I knew what he wanted.   45. I saw . . .   46. When were you leaving . . .   47. The sheep always bleated.   48. You usually ran . . .   49. My father left his car at home when he drank.   50. She went . . .   51. Ben was laughing . . .   52. Mother and I kept . . .   53. Mary was saying . . .   54. Did she tell . . .   55. Were we putting . . .   56. Did I always turn . . . .   57. Was father pointing . . .   58. What did you say . . .   59. Did Robert always watch . . .   60. Did the monkey shake . . .   61. Was I pointing . . .   62. Were you rubbing . . .   63. Why did monkeys always eat . . .   64. Did we always shout . . .   65. Were the babies crying . . .   66. It was . . .   67. Tom saw . . .   68. John came . . .   69. A man and a girl were getting . . .   70. I did . . .   71. Linda showed . . .   72. We always left . . .   73. Peter had . . .   74. We were looking . . .   75. She took . . .   76. Mother went . . .   77. I counted . . .   78. Kate was cutting . . .   79. We put . . .   80. Peter always waited . . .   81. The boys were sleeping . . .   82. They played . . .   83. She wanted . . .   84. We were singing . . .   85. Tom was riding . . .   86. He cleaned . . .   87. Did they take . . .   88. The men were repairing . . .   89. The women helped . . .   90. Mary washed . . .   91. She was ironing . . .   92. Mother and Linda were hanging . . .   93. The children left . . .   94. The monkeys shook . . .   95. John told . . .   96. The keeper was feeding . . .   97. They were eating . . .   98. Did they always eat . . .   99. We were . . .   100. The camel sometimes stood . . .   101. Why were you laughing?   102. Father said . . .   103. Barbara knew how big the baby bear was.   104. You and I were leaving . . .   105. I always bought . . .   106. The elephant was lifting . . .   107. They shook hands when they said . . .   108. We were taking   109. The girls came . . .   110. I had . . .   111. Were you happy when you went . . .   112. Did you like . . .   113. My brother often cried.   114. Monkeys often rubbed . . .   115. Did the people always

Past tense

buy... 116. Were they answering your question then? 117. He held her hand when the wolves howled. 118. They wiped the board when you told... 119. Did he watch you when you were swimming? 120. Their father put... 121. We bought... 122. The people saw... 123. Did you know... 124. Why did the children cry... 125. Mother and I said, "You were shouting... 126. Where were you going... 127. He told them, "You ate..." 128. The girl rubbed her hands because it was cold. 129. When did you get... 130. My mother threw... 131. You were standing... 132. I went... 133. Linda and Mary said... 134. Tina and I were watching... 135. My brother was holding... 136. My father always bought... 137. I sometimes stepped... 138. Helen and Jane were taking... 139. Did your father smoke? 140. My sister and I carried... 141. You often threw... 142. I was playing... 143. Mother and I always fed... 144. Did I talk... 145. Tom went... 146. We helped... 147. Did you collect... 148. They were coming... 149. I was holding... 150. Linda blew... 151. Were you dreaming? 152. Did he eat... 153. Could you come? 154. Did the girls work... 155. That was... 156. The lesson began... 157. We caught... 158. Was he sleeping? 159. I was building... 160. Susan wanted... 161. Jane and Tim liked... 162. Did your dog bite? 163. Could I read... 164. We cut... 165. Tom was swimming. 166. Was I pushing? 167. I hated... 168. You shouted... 169. We stayed in the house when it was hot. 170. Did your aunt ride... 171. The men carried... 172. I worked... 173. The monkey climbed... 174. You talked... 175. Were the Millers flying... 176. My mother was washing... 177. We lived... 178. Was the plane arriving... 179. The flower was growing. 180. Were we picking... 181. My brother called... 182. You were pulling... 183. They could see... 184. Was Diane drawing... 185. You took... 186. Did we know... 187. Tom loved... 188. The man cooked... 189. You looked funny. 190. The baby hurt... 191. My brother and I don't break... 192. Does the cat climb... 193. We like... 194. The dog hurts... 195. I am eating... 196. Do they work... 197. The farmer feeds... 198. We meet... 199. Is father learning... 200. The men don't cut... 201. Do I sometimes drop... 202. Does your sister wash... 203. You are hiding... 204. The woman loves... 205. My father and mother send... 206. Is the dog living... 207. We can talk... 208. I don't help... 209. Your brother often comes... 210. Is the lady drinking... 211. You pick... 212. Does she sing... 213. My father is lighting... 214. Are the girls shouting? 215. Our cat doesn't forget... 216. Do we sweep... 217. My mother doesn't hear... 218. The girl can feel... 219. You don't carry... 220. Am I wearing... 221. Tom and Jean work... 222. My brother reads... 223. Are we collecting... 224. My sister is riding... 225. Are you running... 226. I blow... 227. The cat is shaking... 228. Do you fetch... 229. Do we want... 230. The man doesn't push... 231. Does the girl swim... 232. The dog pulls... 233. The girl doesn't keep... 234. We are selling... 235. Do

Past tense

they stand . . .   236. Does he often call . . .   237. Is your brother buying . . .   238. Her mother doesn't cook . . .   239. The lady gives . . .   240. The women are speaking . . .   241. The doctor arrives . . .   242. Do you cry . . .   243. Is he holding . . .   244. John and Barbara take . . .   245. We are shouting . . .   246. They buy . . .   247. Does he laugh . . .   248. Are you making . . .   249. Yes, I make . . .   250. The dog barks when it sees . . .   251. We always smile . . .   252. You feed. . .   253. Are you pointing . . .   254. Does your brother go . . .   255. Father is helping . . .   256. They are laughing when I see . . .   257. He rushes into a corner when he sees me.   258. Does he smoke . . .   259. The bear shakes its head when it stands . . .   260. We are dancing today.   261. My mother puts . . .   262. I am teasing . . .   263. Do you laugh when Tom tells . . .   264. He is holding his handkerchief when he waves . . .   265. Do I see . . .   266. Does he sometimes carry . . .   267. We hold . . .   268. They come . . .   269. The man leaves . . .   270. Linda and I make . . .   271. Does the lady rush . . .   272. Is the wolf howling?   273. When does the elephant lift . . .   274. Does he leave . . .   275. My brother and sister are standing . . .   276. I am shaking . . .   277. When do you tell . . .   278. That man is taking . . .   279. Don't I keep . . .   280. Are Linda and Sandy walking?   281. My mother and I don't pay for our bread today.   282. I am going . . .   283. They feed . . .   284. Aren't you coming . . .   285. The horse is running . . .   286. I choose . . .   287. Isn't the boy doing . . .   288. Are you helping mother today?   289. Karen and I buy . . .   290. You don't leave . . .   291. I am not shouting . . .   292. Don't the girls stay . . .   293. Is the lady speaking . . .   294. You drink . . .   295. The girl doesn't make . . .   296. Tom and I are eating . . .

Past simple — Past progressive

5. Past simple — Past Progressive

1. She opened the window, looked out, and saw her mother. 2. The dog was barking when I came home. 3. When did I see you last? 4. You were blowing your nose at that moment. 5. He flew to London every week last year. 6. Were they riding a horse at that time yesterday? 7. I often swept the kitchen. 8. While we were sleeping, the dogs were barking. 9. Did you meet her on Mondays? 10. She was singing a song right then. 11. When I saw mother, she was buying bread. 12. He left his house at 10 yesterday morning. 13. I always brought him his book in the morning. 14. We were holding hands when mother came in. 15. Was he feeding the cat at that moment? 16. We were digging a hole for two hours yesterday. 17. Did she always hide her books? 18. You were running too quickly at this time yesterday. 19. Two people were shaking hands when the third person shouted. 20. The cat always slept the whole day in winter. 21. My sister was telling me a story when you came. 22. My mother was reading a book when I phoned yesterday. 23. You always woke me up at 7 o'clock. 24. The children were taking the test for four hours yesterday. 25. Did he learn his vocabulary words yesterday? 26. We usually spread butter on our bread. 27. We were wearing old clothes right then. 28. Was she beginning to talk at that moment? 29. The children grew so quickly last year. 30. The children were running around when the teacher called them. 31. The dog broke its leg when it jumped. 32. The children were freezing in the cold yesterday when I saw them. 33. Did the tree get enough water in summer? 34. Did mother and I come quickly enough yesterday? 35. The lady was lying in bed at that time yesterday. 36. While one girl was reading, the other girl was writing. 37. The woman paid her bills yesterday. 38. Were you standing in the cold while he was taking a bath? 39. The boy was winning the game when I came. 40. We often sold our own clothes. 41. Did the men always show the women their books? 42. They were singing while mother was washing the dishes. 43. I always rang the bell at 5 o'clock. 44. The man and I were speaking for two hours yesterday. 45. You often bit my finger when you were a baby. 46. Was I cutting the cake when you came in? 47. While the boy was running, his sister was sleeping. 48. He always ate too much until he became sick. 49. In the picture she was falling down the steps. 50. Did the men often choose the right toy? 51. Mother was cutting the cake when father came home. 52. Her nose often bled in winter. 53. Were we buying shoes at that time? 54. The men were selling their cars in the picture. 55. You often stole my money! 56. They were driving to Bonn at that moment. 57. Did he always go to the shop in the afternoon? 58. Father and I usually gave the children a book. 59. Two days ago the dog barked, bit the child and ran away. But then we found it. 60. The dog and cat were fighting when I saw them. 61. The girl caught the ball every day. 62. While the man was cooking, his wife was getting everything ready. 63. Did the old man always forget his name? 64. I was feeling sad when you phoned. Now I'm happy. 65. The balloon burst when the child stuck a pin in it. 66. My

Past simple — past progressive

brother and I put our coats on in winter.   67. The boy was still sleeping when we woke up.   68. You were writing letters when I saw you yesterday.   69. Did the teachers teach you to write when you were small?   70. My teacher always let me go home early on Mondays.   71. The child which she heard was crying and was looking for its mother.   72. She always sold flowers in spring.   73. I was digging a hole at that time yesterday.   74. Did the cat sometimes sit in the sun?   75. The man was saying good-bye when you came.   76. We always spent our holiday in Spain.   77. Did I lose my hat yesterday?   78. You were taking a test at that time yesterday.   79. The birds built a nest every year.   80. Was she doing her homework when you came?   81. You sometimes drank milk in the evenings.   82. I was giving a party right then.   83. Were they shaking their heads at that moment?   84. He always spelt his name incorrectly.   85. Yesterday I phoned my sister, packed my things and drove to her house.   86. The cat always caught mice in summer.   87. The painter was drawing a picture when we saw him.   88. Did the girl always find her books in her room?   89. You sometimes bought a blouse when you were in the city.   90. I was fighting a cold at that time last week.
91. The bad boy always stole money from his mother.   92. Were the children hiding when their mother looked for them?   93. You were riding a horse while your sister was washing the car.   94. Did the woman usually sleep so late in the morning?   95. We were standing in the rain at that time.   96. I sometimes lay in bed until 10 in the morning.   97. Did the birds fly to the south in the winter?   98. The teacher was just shutting her book when the pupils came in.   99. The boy always won when he played cards.   100. Did we begin to talk at ten or nine?

6. Question formation in the Past

1. How many houses did he see?   2. Who was eating pudding?   3. Where did I sing a song?   4. How many houses were Mother and I building?   5. Who was writing a letter?   6. Whose apple was I biting?   7. How many words did you write?   8. Why did he give you the present?   9. What were the three girls singing this morning?   10. How did I read the book?   11. When did the little boy know the answer?   12. Where were you sitting?   13. Why did Tom and I run?   14. What did Mother hang up?   15. Why did Linda and Gary ring us up?   16. For whom did Mother buy a cat? / Whom did Mother buy a cat for?   17. Who began to read?   18. How was the cat walking?   19. When were you reading the book?   20. When was the woman selling flowers?   21. With whose balls were the dogs and I playing?   22. How did you eat?   23. How was I working?   24. Where did my brother drive his car?   25. Why did we eat ice-cream?   26. Who shook their heads?   27. Where did you throw the ball?   28. Where was I walking?   29. How many bones were the dogs chewing?   30. What did the little dog catch?   31. Who was flying in a plane?   32. Who went swimming on Sunday?   33. Where did the children take their toys?   34. Why was the baby boy wearing a hat?   35. For how many hours did I swim?   36. Where were the books lying?   37. Who broke the pencil?   38. Why did Linda and Bob hold hands?   39. Whose hand did Father and I hold?   40. Where did the boy find the ball?   41. Where did Mother and I hang the picture up?   42. Where did I go every week?   43. How many apples was the girl buying?   44. Why did Ben and I learn the words?   45. When did you give me a kiss?   46. How did Mother sleep?   47. Where did the cat bring a mouse?   48. What did his uncle carry?   49. When did you go to Bonn?   50. How did the children run?   51. When did my sisters and I meet the man?   52. Why were you smiling?   53. Whose cars were the men selling?   54. Who bought milk?   55. What did you see yesterday?   56. Whose banana did the monkeys eat?   57. When did I feed the cat?   58. How many words did the women and I speak?   59. How were you jumping?   60. Who walked home yesterday?   61. When were the men sweeping the kitchen?   62. Why were the old women sitting down?   63. Where were the children and I riding horses?   64. What did the boy hold?   65. How many books was I reading?   66. Where were the children quiet?   67. What did my father sometimes tell?   68. What was Linda throwing?   69. Where were the men standing?   70. How many balls did the boys throw?   71. Who drew pictures?   72. Who was selling cars?   73. Whose car did you see?   74. To whom were we reading a book?/Who were we reading a book to?   75. Why was I reading the book?   76. When did they have lunch?   77. For whom was Tom cooking?/Whom was Tom cooking for?   78. Whose ball were you catching?   79. When was I making a cake?   80. How did Father and I speak?   81. How were the men working?   82. Where were you walking?   83. How were we driving?   84. What was the elephant holding?   85. Whose book did I take?   86. For whom were Linda and Dick buying toys?/Whom were Linda and Dick buying toys for?   87. Who was driving

Question formation in the Past

home? 88. Where was the cat hiding? 89. Who was driving the car?
90. How did the dogs bark? 91. For whom was I washing the dishes?
92. Whose dog was the man feeding? 93. Who was touching noses?
94. How many lions were you hearing? 95. Who was talking on the phone?
96. When were my father and I drinking milk? 97. Where did I burn my finger?
98. Where did the doctors take sick people? 99. What were we sweeping?
100. Who was writing many sentences?

7. Question formation

1. Who is this?   2. What is she selling?   3. When can you see her?   4. What does she sell?   5. When does she sell the newspaper?   6. What is Mr. Jones?   7. What is he doing?   8. Where does he often drive?   9. Where are Peggy and Jill walking?   10. What do they often do?   11. Do they go to work by bus?   12. Where is Mr. Summers sitting?   13. Does he sometimes watch the children?   14. What does he do?   15. Where can he sleep?   16. Who is driving her car?   17. Where do Mike and Joe live?   18. Are they asking people about their jobs?   19. Who lives in London?   20. What are Mike and Joe doing?   21. When is Mrs. Pritchard closing her shop?   22. What can Mr. Carter catch?   23. When do Mike and Joe get up?   24. Is Mike watching the people?   25. Who can go to work by train?   26. Why does Mr. Jackson drive to London?   27. How many children does Mr. Summer see?   28. Whom does Mrs. Black sell a newspaper?   29. How many girls walk to work?   30. Who watches Mr. Summers?   31. Whose toy did the child take?   32. Where does the man put his coat?   33. Why will the people come?   34. Who was running to the bus?   35. Why is he cutting your hair?   36. Whom have you seen often?   37. What are you blowing up?   38. Who/What caught a ball?   39. Whom/What was the lady holding yesterday?   40. What does my brother do every day?   41. What will their parents hear?   42. Who goes to church every Sunday?   43. Whom do you take to a show every week?   44. Where can my brothers dash after school?   45. Is my sister buying a new car?   46. What did we do yesterday?   47. Whose sister has washed his shirts?   48. Whose sister do we ring up every day?   49. When must the children go to school?   50. When must my father wake Mother up?   51. Was I riding the pony when you saw me? / Wasn't I riding the pony when you saw me? / Were you riding the pony when I saw you? / Weren't you riding the pony when I saw you?   52. What is Linda holding?   53. What did the men do?   54. Does the bird eat from his hand?   55. Who sees many dogs?   56. What were Jim and I taking?   57. When have they taken a trip?   58. What/Whom is Mr. Smith holding?   59. Who/What drinks milk?   60. Why did Bob and Mary run home?   61. Whose coat was blue?   62. With whom will I walk home tomorrow?/ With whom will you walk home tomorrow?   63. Are you helping me now? / Am I helping you now?   64. Where are you walking? / Where am I walking?   65. Who was eating an apple?   66. What were Linda and I/you taking?   67. Can he help you/me today?   68. What were Mother and I/you holding?   69. How many girls do I/you always see?   70. Did Mary go to the supermarket?   71. When did the boy see the bird?   72. Does the dog bark often?   73. With whom is Mr. Smith talking?   74. How many books will you/I read tomorrow?   75. With whom are we/you walking?   76. Whom should we/you help?   77. Who is talking to her sister?   78. Who is here?   79. When will we/you run to school?   80. Where did he run after lunch?   81. Who throws balls every day?   82. What have they given her?   83. Why am I happy?/Why are you happy?   84. How often did they speak to her?   85. How many trees were growing near the river?   86. What did the mon-

Question formation

key do?   87. Where are we/you hiding?   88. When did we/you drink milk?   89. What did they take?   90. How many books did she buy?   91. Why did I/you tell you/me a story?   92. Who stood in the church?   93. Where did he go?   94. What do they eat?   95. Who ran home?   96. When did I/you go swimming?   97. Why did you/I help me/you?   98. How many girls bought books?   99. Where were we/you flying a kite?   100. Who can help you/me?   101. When will we/you be visiting them?   102. Do you like him?   103. What does he eat every day?   104. When will she call him?   105. When did Mother go to Bonn?   106. With whom will we/you talk tomorrow?   107. Did Don take his coat with him?   108. Where are you/am I running?   109. How many apples do I/you always eat every week?   110. What do I/you see?   111. Who has cars?   112. When did the shop close?   113. Can I/you come to visit you/me?   114. Where are they walking?   115. Whom is he looking at?/At whom is he looking?   116. How often did I/you sing that song?   117. What does she often do?   118. Did they wear hats yesterday?   119. What did they buy last week?   120. How did she run?   121. Why did he hide behind a curtain?   122. Where will she go tomorrow?   123. What did we/you listen to? / To what did we/you listen?   124. How many children are running down the street?   125. What did they always do?   126. Who forgot to take his umbrella?   127. Why had they given her two pounds?   128. When will you/I be driving there?   129. What has she done?   130. How many pieces of cake does he eat every day?   131. Where did we/you swim?   132. When are you/am I buying a new coat?   133. Who speaks to me every day?   134. a. Who saw the birds on the tree?   b. How many boys saw the birds on the tree?   c. What did the three boys see on the tree?   d. Where did the three boys see the birds?   135. a. Who is sitting on the chair?   b. Whose sister is sitting on the chair?   c. Where is father's sister sitting?   136. a. Whom do we/you always give books to read?   b. What do we/you aways give you/us to read?   137. a. Who was eating apples in the garage?   b. What were the boys eating in the garage?   c. Where were the boys eating apples?   138. a. Who will buy Susan five new books?   b. Whom will father buy five new books?   c. How many new books will father buy Susan?   d. What will father buy Susan?   139. a. Whose daughter took Mike's car?   b. What did the Miller's daughter take?   c. Whose car did the Miller's daughter take?   140. a. Where do they go every summer?   b. When do they go to Rome?   141. a. Who was sitting on a chair in the kitchen?   b. How many boys were sitting on a chair in the kitchen?   c. On what were three boys sitting in the kitchen?   d. Where were three boys sitting on a chair?   e. What were three boys doing?   142. a. Who sees four trees?   b. What does he see?   c. How many trees does he see?   143. a. Who is going to Berlin tomorrow?   b. Where am I/are you going tomorrow?   c. When am I/are you going to Berlin?   d. What am I/are you doing tomorrow?   144. a. Who wrote twenty letters yesterday?   b. Whose sister wrote twenty letters yesterday?   c. What did Jane's sister write yesterday?   d. When did Jane's sister write twenty letters?   e. What did Jane's sister do yesterday?   145. a. How long did they talk today?   b. When did they talk for two hours?   c. What did they do today?   146. a. Who will go to the beach next week?

Question formation 17

b. Where will the class go next week?   c. When will the class go to the beach?   d. What will the class do next week?   147. a. Who helps me/you every day?   b. Whose brother helps me/you every day?   c. Whom does John's brother help every day?   d. When does John's brother help me/you?   e. What does John's brother do every day?   148. a. Who is playing football?   b. How many boys are playing football?   c. What are two boys playing?   149. a. What/Who saw our dog yesterday?   b. Whose dog did the lion see yesterday?   c. What did the lion see yesterday?   d. When did the lion see our dog?   150. a. Who always eats six bars of chocolate?   b. How many girls always eat six bars of chocolate?   c. How many bars of chocolate do the three girls always eat?   d. What do the three girls always eat?   e. What do the three girls always do?   151. a. Who can help you tomorrow?   b. Whom can mother and I help tomorrow?   c. When can mother and I help you?   d. What can mother and I do?   152. a. Whose brother will go to school?   b. Who will go to school?   c. Where will my brother go?   d. What will my brother do?   153. a. Who is throwing a ball?   b. What is the girl throwing?   c. What is the girl doing?   154. a. Who often laughs at his brother?   b. What does the boy often do?   155. a. Who was writing sentences?   b. What were the men writing?   c. What were the men doing?   156. a. Who said a word?   b. What did mother say?   c. What did mother do?   157. a. Who will read a book tomorrow?   b. What will father read tomorrow?   c. When will father read a book?   d. What will father do tomorrow?   158. a. Is father reading?   159. a. Who always reads books?   b. What does father always read?   c. What does father always do?   160. a. Who often read books when he was a boy?   b. What did father often read when he was a boy?   c. When did father often read books?   d. What did father often do when he was a boy?   e. What did father often do?   161. a. Who often washes our/his cars?   b. What do we/you often wash?   c. What do we/you often do?   162. Did he usually read them?   163. Was he reading a book? / Wasn't he reading a book?   164. a. Who is writing a letter?   b. What are you writing?   165. Did you write one yesterday?   166. What do mother and I always eat on Sunday?   167. Will we give you the paper?   168. What do my father and mother often do?   169. Where are we running?   170. Where did Lois and Terry buy that?   171. What can the keeper feed?   172. What did they do yesterday?   173. Can he swim well? / Can't he swim well?   174. Why is Linda sitting there?   175. When was I wearing a coat?   176. Do father and mother drive a car? / Don't father and mother drive a car?   177. Who is standing at the window?   178. At how many boys did my brother throw the books?   179. When were you wearing a blouse?   180. Whom have they taken to church?   181. How many boys wrote a letter?   182. Who rings them up every evening?   183. What do we do every afternoon?   184. With whose brother has mother spoken?   185. Whose sister told me a story?   186. What do Tom and Carol always eat at school?   187. Can you/we give me/you that book? / Can't you/we give me/you that book?   188. What will the keeper feed?   189. Where are they running?   190. What did the monkeys do?   191. When did mother and I/you go to the shop?   192. What were my brothers singing?   193. Will his sister swim next week?   194. What does my sister hear

Question formation

every morning? 195. Does my/your brother drink coffee? / Doesn't my/your brother drink coffee? 196. Who was running after the burglars? 197. Where did the dog chase me? 198. Whom does the man take along in his car? 199. Why do I/you hate that music? 200. Who always carries my/your books? 201. Whom do I/you kiss on her cheek? 202. When did the three birds fly? 203. Why was the child crying? 204. What is the man driving? 205. Who is washing the dishes? 206. Where does the girl work? 207. When do the children go swimming? 208. Why didn't we/you want to sit there? 209. What did the girls take? 210. Where do I/you ride a horse? 211. When is mother flying to Berlin? 212. Whom did the lady give an apple? 213. Why is his boy helping him? 214. Who is cleaning the windows? 215. What do the cats always chase? 216. Where is Jerry sleeping? 217. What is the boy eating? 218. To whom does the baby walk? / Whom does the baby walk to? 219. Who brought his coat? 220. What are Linda and Tom picking? 221. When were the men playing football? 222. Where was I/were you eating a cake? 223. When does the baby cry? 224. Who/What plays on the floor? 225. Whom are you/am I telling a story? 226. Why did Ted and I/you want to go swimming? 227. What did the lady drink? 228. Where were the three children playing? 229. What was barking at the burglar?

Past — Present Perfect

8. Past — Present Perfect

1. visited 2. met 3. did not play 4. Have you ever seen 5. have never seen 6. had 7. has just given 8. broke 9. came, broke 10. have you played 11. fed 12. wrote 13. repaired 14. went 15. have just bought 16. has written 17. did not see 18. have you polished 19. has he written 20. Did you see 21. Have you often seen 22. Didn't I see 23. Have I already eaten 24. did not sleep 25. Haven't we seen 26. has he been waiting 27. did I buy 28. have not spoken 29. have not done 30. took 31. Have we answered 32. Did you see 33. Haven't I seen 34. were playing 35. bought 36. Didn't he visit 37. haven't played 38. Did we eat 39. Was I 40. Didn't he ride 41. flew 42. Didn't I work 43. Didn't you drive 44. Did the lady go 45. Did I do 46. have been working 47. Haven't you ever seen 48. Hasn't he seen 49. Did they sit 50. has been wearing 51. Did you go 52. Has it eaten 53. You did not watch 54. have not seen 55. did he go 56. Didn't we see 57. went 58. Haven't they taken 59. have already fed 60. Has my sister gone 61. did not go 62. Haven't you seen 63. Did father and mother go 64. have never seen 65. did not eat 66. Have you ever heard 67. saw 68. did we drive 69. has been sleeping 70. Didn't they phone 71. Haven't we read 72. have never stolen 73. have just gone 74. stole 75. Have you already brushed 76. did not buy 77. Have I ever seen 78. saw 79. did not see 80. have not read 81. did they live 82. Haven't I greeted 83. went 84. Haven't they just come 85. did not run 86. was not talking 87. Were you reading 88. were not playing 89. Haven't you taken 90. Haven't we eaten 91. did not sleep 92. have been watching 93. has never been 94. did not drive 95. have not seen 96. Were you sleeping 97. wasn't 98. has not written 99. Haven't they gone 100. did not wash

9. Verb tenses

1. had been sleeping   2. had written   3. will have broken   4. Have you been   5. were drinking   6. would not always steal   7. usually drive   8. would have bitten   9. usually caught   10. had sometimes had   11. sleeps   12. always understood   13. Has he got   14. Was the wind blowing   15. have spoken   16. had left   17. will meet   18. was blowing   19. would have forgotten   20. would keep   21. will have begun   22. bought   23. are sleeping   24. fall   25. were riding   26. Have we spoken   27. had had   28. are riding   29. have sometimes got   30. were holding   31. will have begun   32. ate   33. would steal   34. often understood   35. heard   36. have been   37. take   38. was drinking   39. flies   40. am reading   41. was driving   42. was selling   43. had often left   44. is driving   45. were eating   46. call   47. caught   48. got   49. had always had   50. goes   51. will be singing, meet   52. had found, would have given   53. have been speaking   54. caught, could eat / would be able to eat   55. has not seen   56. would be riding   57. was running, had to talk   58. Are you drawing   59. will know, hear   60. were saying, could build / were able to build   61. have slept, will get up   62. had been swimming   63. would buy   64. Is David taking   65. collect, collects   66. goes   67. have just seen   68. was sitting, saw   69. watch, are listening   70. had helped, would have got   71. come, will hear   72. knew, would understand, have said   73. have been talking   74. had hoped, would be writing, came   75. will be drinking, find   76. would have been burning, had not caught   77. was doing, said, would play   78. had talked, had to go, could finish   79. heard, said, will be   80. Have you seen. .   81. had spoken, would have known   82. take, will make   83. will be leaving   84. bought, would eat   85. did not buy   86. does not like. .   87. will have cleaned, come   88. thought, had seen   89. has been swimming   90. had not eaten   91. had given   92. strikes   93. has grown   94. have been flying   95. was putting, saw   96. am lying   97. drew   98. opened, had taken   99. forgets, will sleep   100. are repairing   101. saw, had been learning   102. has, will buy   103. had learnt, would have had   104. has done, is playing   105. was washing, rang   106. ran, would catch   107. come, will build   108. come, will have drawn   109. came   110. were doing   111. had helped, went   112. had read, would have known   113. arrived, was telling   114. run   115. Does your cat run   116. Was he drinking   117. did not catch   118. buys   119. Did you know   120. does not understand   121. takes   122. will have left   123. Did you see   124. is not cleaning   125. Was he cleaning   126. walk   127. Are you taking   128. has taught   129. Does your dog bite   130. has not taught   131. Was, were   132. eats   133. had not written   134. does not like   135. Is your mother making   136. saw   137. have already asked   138. Were the girls singing   139. His father has given   140. Does he drink   141. sometimes smoke   142. were eating   143. would have eaten, had found   144. always carries   145. often feeds   146. would cut   147. Would your sister know, met   148. will hide   149. Can he drive / Is he able to drive   150. had

Verb tenses

caught, would have thrown   151. usually thought   152. will be holding   153. would have eaten, had kept   154. does not usually drive   155. Would you eat, bought   156. does not usually speak   157. sometimes brought   158. feeds   159. Would he sell, drew   160. were shutting   161. Will you be wearing   162. will they have read   163. spent, will go   164. is driving   165. bought   166. will often draw   167. heard   168. were selling   169. Has she spoken   170. goes   171. Did you play   172. is   173. has already started   174. were washing   175. arrrested   176. is studying   177. did you arrive   178. has been crying   179. have known   180. left   181. had to talk   182. were still talking   183. has always worked   184. will go   185. don't want   186. lives   187. has helped   188. is burning   189. saw   190. caught   191. has been raining   192. Is your father working   193. am trying   194. is talking   195. has not seen   196. taught   197. was still working   198. broke   199. has broken   200. were not wearing   201. was washing   202. did not visit   203. has been playing   204. phoned   205. are reading   206. met   207. went, bought   208. is helping   209. go   210. has been working, began   211. sings   212. will have fed   213. spent   214. drinks, drank   215. have been writing   216. have been playing   217. would buy   218. has never eaten   219. would have driven   220. am taking   221. will fly / will be flying   222. will have shut   223. Haven't you written   224. would read   225. were drawing   226. had already found   227. will meet   228. were stealing   229. could sweep / were able to sweep   230. will swim   231. have been sweeping   232. would hide   233. is brushing   234. have been reading   235. would have worn   236. has never torn   237. Haven't you found   238. lost, Have you seen. . 239. have not seen   240. Did you watch   241. have not heard, got   242. got, was   243. has just moved   244. have you been   245. Did he see   246. saw   247. Will you read   248. will not read / won't read   249. gave   250. came   251. was not / wasn't   252. have known   253. told   254. has never forgotten   255. is swimming   256. would drink   257. have taught   258. was buying   259. Have they ever sold   260. did not learn   261. have been sitting   262. will have begun   263. have sung   264. are biting   265. flies   266. Are you leaving   267. has never written   268. did not hear   269. had to drive   270. were   271. Have you ever stuck   272. Did she play   273. have been doing   274. had already paid   275. did not pay   276. will hide   277. were holding   278. has that man shaken   279. has been teaching   280. would put   281. could feed / were able to feed   282. will be building   283. had to catch   284. has never made   285. have been standing   286. are running   287. could throw / was able to throw   288. will see   289. did not go   290. will be holding   291. b.   292. c.   293. a.   294. d.   295. b.   296. a.   297. d.   298. c.   299. b.   300. a.

10. Comparison of adjectives

1. smaller   2. the largest   3. happier   4. more exciting   5. the most interesting   6. cool   7. more helpful   8. noisier   9. the eldest / the oldest   10. more   11. softer   12. the highest   13. bright   14. taller   15. the most thrilling   16. more careful   17. the most expensive   18. stronger   19. beautiful   20. the widest   21. more interesting   22. the farthest   23. warmer   24. stupid   25. the most important   26. uglier   27. the rainiest   28. sweet   29. juicier   30. old   31. the quickest   32. later   33. polite   34. prettier   35. the worst   36. sicker   37. the hungriest   38. fewer   39. more thrilling   40. better   41. the loudest   42. more reliable   43. good   44. more musical   45. the oldest   46. more useful   47. the youngest   48. more furious   49. expensive   50. cleaner   51. the brightest   52. more complicated   53. clever   54. more active   55. the most   56. worse   57. bad   58. more handsome   59. many   60. more important   61. the thickest   62. more severe / severer   63. bad   64. more difficult   65. the cleverest / the most clever   66. more exciting   67. important   68. more expensive   69. little   70. the friendliest / the most friendly   71. less   72. colourful   73. the simplest / the most simple   74. more ambitious   75. far   76. more unpleasant   77. the quietest / the most quiet   78. terrible   79. more comfortable   80. farther   81. the most attractive   82. younger   83. famous   84. more   85. the best   86. faster   87. the craziest   88. older   89. modern   90. hotter   91. happy   92. more sincere / sincerer   93. more gentle / gentler   94. the least   95. more common / commoner   96. more popular   97. the strongest   98. more stupid / stupider   99. smaller   100. the most nervous   101. more friendly / friendlier   102. the most generous   103. the dirtiest   104. the most curious   105. fresh   106. more attentive   107. tidy   108. the proudest   109. pleasant   110. busier

If-clauses

11. If-clauses

1. were   2. could have helped   3. takes   4. will give   5. does not speak   6. would have come   7. would know   8. will repair   9. would have won   10. did not know   11. have   12. would help   13. would have shot   14. will invite   15. will you do   16. would he do   17. would go   18. would we have done   19. could not have come   20. would you do   21. would have drunk   22. does not hurry   23. would have missed   24. will you do   25. spoke   26. did not speak   27. would have spoken   28. would have come   29. could they give   30. did not eat   31. would help   32. drives   33. saw   34. will run   35. will have to pay   36. had had   37. would they have gone   38. could have held   39. see   40. give   41. had caught   42. found   43. had not thrown   44. will he be able to come   45. would be   46. could have driven   47. will have to go   48. would they have hidden   49. did not feed   50. teaches   51. would have written   52. would you buy   53. would have flown   54. had seen   55. had asked   56. sees   57. ate   58. would read   59. saw   60. would I have found   61. would have given   62. could have eaten   63. help   64. will he go   65. had heard   66. would you be able to eat / could you eat   67. did not live   68. would be   69. would have seen   70. had turned on   71. will have to wait   72. catches   73. did not talk   74. could have visited   75. had helped   76. could he win / would he be able to win   77. will be able to catch / can catch   78. had taken   79. would have gone   80. runs   81. ran   82. would have shaken   83. will they come   84. would pay   85. catch   86. would she have drunk   87. did not speak   88. would see   89. will get   90. would have bought   91. will be able to go / can go   92. gives   93. would have been   94. had known   95. had found   96. would eat   97. flew   98. would have given   99. bought   100. will scream   101. could show / would be able to show   102. had gone   103. will come   104. left   105. could have read / would have been able to read   106. hears   107. could have hurt   108. would not be   109. do not eat   110. can drive / is able to drive   111. had known   112. ran   113. will drive   114. did not have   115. would have said   116. would have had to eat   117. would see   118. will have to talk   119. would be   120. eats   121. had found   122. would you go   123. would have brought   124. threw   125. brings   126. asks   127. likes   128. would she buy   129. had played   130. tried   131. would have had   132. had seen   133. will eat   134. had   135. would have had to drive   136. can catch / is able to catch   137. must phone / will have to phone   138. did not have   139. would have taken   140. do not take   141. would open   142. can use / is able to use   143. do not see   144. would have read   145. came   146. would have played   147. would have had to help   148. would run   149. had had   150. will have to give   151. had come   152. would she use   153. was / were   154. buys   155. did not know   156. takes   157. will call   158. would have read   159. did not talk   160. would buy   161. will laugh   162. would have taken   163. would they sing   164. hides   165. held   166. had seen   167. will have to say / must say

If-clauses

168. can help   169. would have had to pay   170. do not bring   171. saw   172. comes   173. does not shut   174. will hear   175. would wear   176. drank   177. had allowed   178. bleeds   179. would shout   180. was / were   181. does not wake   182. would not have been   183. will phone   184. would cover   185. would have had   186. rises   187. had caught   188. does not hide   189. would not have fallen   190. will have   191. knelt   192. lets   193. had not broken   194. would ring   195. He could have helped you if he had wanted to.   196. If you gave him the book now, he could translate it.   197. If I were you, I would wash my hands.   198. He would still have got (caught) the train if he had found his ticket.   199. If he comes late, we will not go to the cinema.   200. I would have given Paul the letter if I had seen him.   201. If we did that, he would be happy.   202. I would see Susan if I went to school.   203. If we had seen the letter, we would have read it.   204. If he sees the cake, he will eat it.   205. If he had seen Linda, he would have given her money.   206. If I see him, I will give him the letter.   207. We would have gone soon if we had not come so late.   208. I would have helped father if I had seen him.   209. If the woman came, we would laugh.   210. If we visit them (her), we will take a flower along.   211. If they sell the house, they will get much money.   212. If I had seen the children, I would have laughed.   213. If the man were here, he would help me.   214. If he had been at home, he would have caught the burglar.   215. If you come, you will see my horses.   216. If I stop now, I can go to bed.   217. If I were you, I would go to bed.   218. If she had gone to bed earlier, she would not have been so tired.   219. If you go to the doctor, you will not like it.   220. If we had found the camera, we would have taken pictures.   221. I could have helped her if she had asked.   222. He would speak with us if we phoned him.   223. If they come, we will drink coffee.   224. We would write letters if we had pencils.   225. If you hide, we will find you.   226. He would have been able to give you the chair if he had known it. / He could have given you the chair if he had known it.   227. If I had slept long, I would not have been so tired.   228. We could have driven there if the weather had been better.   229. If I had seen you, I would have been happy.   230. You would sleep if you had beds.   231. If he shows us the picture, we will show him our pictures, too.   232. I would bake a cake if I had sugar.   233. If we help him, it will go much quicker.   234. If he had bought that, he would have been unhappy.   235. They could have seen the king if they had come sooner. / They would have been able to see the king if they had come sooner.

Question tags

12. Question Tags

1. hasn't he   2. aren't they   3. does he   4. is it   5. has he   6. can't she   7. is he   8. don't they   9. will she   10. wouldn't they   11. don't we   12. can't we   13. had we   14. was I   15. aren't you   16. didn't she   17. did we   18. are they   19. would he   20. don't we   21. haven't I   22. have you   23. won't we   24. will you   25. aren't they   26. would she   27. won't you   28. doesn't he   29. would we   30. weren't you   31. are they   32. wouldn't we   33. did he   34. aren't you   35. can they   36. haven't I   37. are you   38. won't she   39. can we   40. didn't I   41. are they   42. wouldn't I   43. do we   44. were you   45. hasn't he   46. did it   47. wouldn't we   48. will you   49. wouldn't I   50. aren't they   51. have we   52. weren't you   53. hadn't she   54. would we   55. did you   56. weren't they   57. do I   58. will he   59. did we   60. am I   61. wouldn't it   62. have we   63. wouldn't you   64. hadn't I   65. could they   66. hadn't we   67. had you   68. did she   69. wouldn't he   70. have they   71. aren't we   72. had it   73. won't you   74. could I   75. haven't they   76. do you   77. will we   78. can't it   79. did you   80. wouldn't they   81. will I   82. does she   83. wouldn't you   84. were they   85. don't I   86. would he   87. haven't you   88. haven't we   89. do I   90. will they   91. didn't we   92. has he   93. hadn't you   94. does he   95. won't they   96. did you   97. can he   98. couldn't she   99. would they   100. don't you   101. won't you   102. had you   103. isn't he   104. hasn't it   105. doesn't he   106. would she   107. hadn't we   108. wouldn't you   109. will they   110. wouldn't I   111. did I   112. hasn't he

13. Relative Clauses

1. whose   2. which   3. who   4. whom   5. whose   6. whom   7. which   8. whom
9. whose   10. whom   11. which   12. whom   13. whose   14. which   15. who
16. whom   17. who   18. whom   19. whose   20. which   21. which
22. which   23. who   24. who   25. which 26. whom   27. which   28. whom
29. whose   30. which   31. who   32. which   33. whose   34. who
35. which   36. who   37. whose 38. whom   39. whose   40. we visited
41. we drank with our meal   42. we stayed at   43. we slept in   44. who has ten children   45. who filled a sack with their best apples   46. which Sam carried   47. they looked at   48. who was walking by himself   49. the two brothers were taking to market   50. we live in   51. we saw on the street   52. we ate from   53. who was walking through a street in London, which had dresses in it.   54. he saw   55. whose shop it was   56. he had been talking to   57. mother worked in   58. who wanted to buy the dress mother had put in the window, mother had put in the window   59. whose friend talked to her   60. whom they could give the money to, whose coat was on a chair   61. they had heard of, they had given him   62. we worked in   63. we had gone to   64. whose bicycle was broken   65. we had heard   66. who was combing her hair   67. Peter whom he had helped said "thank you." / He had helped Peter who said "thank you."
68. The pictures which we were looking at were interesting. / We were looking at the pictures which were interesting.   69. Mrs. Green whose house we lived in invited Tom to lunch. / Mrs. Green in whose house we lived invited Tom to lunch.
70. The man who ate a cake is here.   71. We took the apple which was lying on the table.   72. Linda whom they had taken home waved good-bye.   73. You could see Mr. Twain whose books Ken has read.   74. We could talk to the lady who was typing a letter.   75. The dog whose ear was hurt could not hear.   76. We saw the boys whom you had played with. / We saw the boys with whom you had played. / We saw the boys you had played with.   77. Dick whom we had brought home said "hello."   78. You can speak to Linda who is reading the newspaper.
79. They saw Mary Ann and me whom Father played with. / They saw Mary Ann and me with whom Father played.   80. The songs which we were listening to were funny. / The songs to which we were listening were funny. / The songs we were listening to were funny.   81. The woman who has eaten an apple is there.
82. Linda has stolen the money which was lying under the chair.   83. We waved at the Beatles whose records Tom has heard.   84. The cat whose eye is bad cannot see.   85. Peter and Sue whom Jenny helped said "thank you."   86. Mr. Black whose house we live in will invite Laurie to dinner. / Mr. Black in whose house we live will invite Laurie to dinner.   87. John is running to his brother who gave him the bicycle.   88. Mr. Green whose shop is in Cologne sells many things.
89. They drive along the street which is very busy.   90. Uncle John whom Bob helps with the work eats fish every day.   91. That is the man who took my car which is 5 years old.   92. The man whom I see is eating a sandwich. / The man I see is eating a sandwich.   93. The girl who is my sister always combs her hair.

Relative Clauses

94. The dog which is running down the street is black. 95. The balcony which I am sitting on is blue. / The balcony on which I am sitting is blue. / The balcony I am sitting on is blue. 96. I am reading the letter which is from my father. 97. The little boy whom my mother is holding is crying. / The little boy my mother is holding is crying. 98. The man whose car I drove gave me a book. 99. The woman whose husband stood up was talking then. 100. The child whose arm was broken cried. 101. The dog whose tail was wagging was happy. 102. The man whose coat was torn talked to me. 103. The girl whose birthday it was was happy. 104. The boy who had his own coat ran home. 105. The man whom I gave the book to is my father. / The man to whom I gave the book is my father. / The man I gave the book to is my father. 106. His sister whom he bought a present for is 32. / His sister for whom he bought a present is 32. 107. The refrigerator which ice-cream was in felt warm. / The refrigerator in which ice-cream was felt warm. 108. The store he was walking to was closed. / The store to which he was walking was closed. / The store which he was walking to was closed. 109. The lady he was talking with had a book. / The lady with whom he was talking had a book. / The lady whom he was talking with had a book. 110. The tables which the chairs were between were painted red. / The tables between which the chairs were were painted red. / The tables the chairs were between were painted red. 111. The table the man was lying on was at the doctor's. / The table which the man was lying on was at the doctor's. / The table on which the man was lying was at the doctor's. 112. A man who was a police officer questioned her. 113. The woman who was his mother rang him up. 114. The man who is very good drives a Mercedes. 115. A building which was very old burnt down last night. 116. The letter which wasn't very important disappeared. 117. The man they've arrested robbed the bank. / The man whom they've arrested robbed the bank. 118. The man she married gave her a ring. / The man whom she married gave her a ring. 119. The money he took was on the table. / The money which he took was on the table. 120. The man I know did this. / The man whom I know did this. 121. I ate the food which made me sick. 122. We had been waiting for the bus which was full. 123. The knife we cut our bread with is sharp. / The knife which we cut our bread with is sharp. / The knife with which we cut our bread is sharp. 124. I was talking to the girl who was my cousin. 125. The man who is my father is nice. / The man who is nice is my father. 126. John is talking to his sister who asked him to come home. 127. The chair was expensive. I sat on the chair. 128. He likes the girl. The girl's mother is now talking. 129. The man is our uncle. We took the books to the man. 130. Can you see the lady? The lady is helping Jane. 131. We helped the lady. The lady's car had stopped. 132. They talked to the lady. He had taken a banana from the lady. 133. The lady ran away. The lady was looking at the dress when I saw her. 134. Penny walked to her mother. I was reading Penny's book. 135. The boy threw the ball. They had seen the boy playing football. 136. The animal was an antelope. The animal had eaten the flower. 137. The baby had no mother. They heard the baby crying. 138. The person was Tom. I had seen the person. 139. The man was father. I

Relative Clauses

had helped the man. 140. The animal was a lion. The animal had left its cage. 141. Rosemary ran to her father. I have found Rosemary's letter. 142. We spoke with the man. You had taken a book from the man. 143. The shoes were new. She had the shoes on. 144. Rita went to the man. The man's car was broken. 145. The man walked away. The man was looking at the car when we saw him. 146. The girl gave me a kiss. You had watched the girl playing with dolls. 147. The girl was sad. The girl's mother had left the house. 148. If I had the camera, I would take a photo. You gave me the camera. 149. The man was his father. He gave the book to the man. 150. The woman carried two books. I saw the woman. 151. The bird cried for help. The bird's tail was in the cat's mouth. 152. If they knew the man, they would tell their mother. The man had phoned. 153. The men ate their lunch. They were working with the men. 154. The people asked me questions. You showed the picture to the people. 155. If he had understood the lady, he would have told his mother. The lady had called. 156. The shop had a fire yesterday. I bought the furniture from the shop. 157. The girl waved to you. The girl was looking at you. 158. The man turned around. I saw the man walking down the street. 159. The book told about cats. She was reading the book when you came. 160. The radio is now broken. We were listening to the radio today. 161. If I wore the dress, I would make her happy. She sold me the dress. 162. He likes the girl. The girl's mother is now talking. 163. Is the man our uncle? We took the books to the man. 164. Can you see the lady? The lady is helping Jane. 165. The inspector wrote down our names. We had spoken with the inspector. 166. Did the cat catch a mouse? The cat's kittens were lapping milk. 167. Were the babies hungry? The babies were crying. 168. We heard the girls. The girls' mothers had gone shopping. 169. The store cost much money. We had bought the store. 170. The horses walked slowly. We rode the horses. 171. Why did the dog bark? He was holding the dog. 172. Didn't you see the man? The man gave me the camera. 173. Did the ball roll away? She was playing with the ball. 174. Have you seen the letters? They've written the letters. 175. When'll the road be finished? They're building the road. 176. Isn't that the biggest fish? We've caught the fish. 177. Did the cat lick him? He fed the cat. 178. Won't you be staying at the house? They live in the house. 179. What was the day like? You longed for the day. 180. Where's the book? She's been reading the book. 181. The plants grew quickly. They gave us the plants. 182. Didn't he hear the noise? The dog made the noise. 183. Will the picture be beautiful? They're drawing the picture.

14. Passive

1. Letters are written by me.   2. A book was written by him.   3. A picture will be drawn by her.   4. The light has been found by him.   5. A friend will be met by you.   6. Her house had been sold (by her.)   7. His letters were torn up (by him.)   8. A radio has been stolen by the man.   9. The car is usually driven by the lady.   10. Bob is beaten by the cook.   11. The thief was caught by the policeman.   12. --   13. The shop is visited by professors.   14. A letter has been written by Linda.   15. I had been met at the station by some friends.   16. The ball is always blown up by Jim.   17. The boys were waited for by the man.   18. Such a song had never been heard of by the girls.   19. All the cake has just been eaten up by the boys and girls.   20. The monkey was laughed at by the children.   21. The boy was looked after by an old man.   22. The project was talked about for a long time (by people.)   23. The lions are fed at noon by the keeper.   24. Yesterday they were fed at noon by him.   25. The water is carried to a higher place by pumps.   26. He was expected to come at three o'clock (by us.)   27. The house is carefully cleaned by Jim.   28. The walls are beautifully painted by Betty.   29. The baby has been cared for every day by Mac.   30. The curtains had been washed well by John.   31. A lecture will be given next week by the doctor.   32. The injured man was taken to the hospital (by the doctor.)   33. He is called Ted by his friends.   34. All the bread has been eaten by the mice.   35. Our windows will be cleaned tomorrow by the man.   36. Those letters will be typed by the secretary.   37. A new edition of the book is now being printed (by them.)   38. He is being visited in hospital by many people.   39. Fruit was being stolen from the apple trees by thieves.   40. The lady at the counter was seen by my father.   41. His books are brought to school by the boy.   42. Her sums have been done by the girl.   43. The next book will be found more interesting (by you.)   44. Seven languages were spoken by the clever man.   45. The ball had been thrown quickly by Bob.   46. Eight words will now be written by me.   47. Many fingers are pointed at Tom by the old women.   48. The lady at the counter was helped by him.   49. The clothes were hung up by the boy.   50. Much money is given to the church by him.   51. The setting sun has been seen by the old man.   52. Bad words had been spoken by him.   53. The train was stopped by robbers.   54. The suitcases are being packed by his wife.   55. Police officers have often been seen by them.   56. The money had been found by a little girl.   57. Birds are fed by many people.   58. My hand will be held by my boyfriend.   59. The men were being watched by the little girl.   60. Letters were written by two friends.   61. That book has been read by the teachers.   62. Apples are eaten every day by my sister.   63. The ball has often been thrown by the boys.   64. Will the letter be opened by the men?   65. Her father and mother are helped by the little girl.   66. Their children would be driven home by the farmers.   67. The doors had been shut by the doctor.   68. The cars were stolen (by you.)   69. A dress is often worn (by you.)   70. A picture is being painted by the artist.   71. Our radio was being repaired by them.

Passive

72. The windows will have been cleaned by this afternoon (by her.)   73. His table is being sold by them.   74. The books had often been found (by you.)   75. The book can be read (by me.)   76. When was the milk drunk by the boy?   77. New balls are being thrown by my brother.   78. A car had been driven by us yesterday.   79. Was a table bought (by them)?   80. The cake will have been eaten by tomorrow (by you.)   81. How will the street be found (by them)?   82. A ball must be blown up by my sister.   83. The dishes would have been broken (by you.)   84. ---   85. Where is your money hidden (by you)?   86. A song was being sung by my sisters.   87. Why will those books be kept (by them)?   88. A book was being hidden by my brothers.   89. ---   90. The forks will have been put away by tomorrow (by us.)   91. I would have been bitten by the dog.   92. A cake must be brought by Linda.   93. Where are such clothes bought (by you)?   94. Was a chair broken (by them)?   95. The ball would be bought by my father.   96. A pen had been found (by them) yesterday   97. When was the man eaten by the lion?   98. A new dress is being worn by my mother.   99. Where are such pictures seen (by you)?   100. A nice song would be heard by the man.   101. ---   102. Was a car driven (by them)?   103. A new car was being bought by father and mother.   104. An answer will have been found by tomorrow (by us.)   105. A big cake is being eaten by my sister.   106. Why will the cat be bitten (by him)?   107. A dress had been worn yesterday (by my sister.)   108. Chairs would have been brought (by us.)   109. When was the book put on the shelf by the lady?   110. The ball must be caught (by them.)   111. The plates will be taken to mother (by me.)   112. Are his cats fed by the boy?   113. Coffee was being drunk by the men.   114. My cold would certainly be caught by the babies.   115. Have the presents been bought by mother?   116. Were the tables being carried by the children?   117. The two patients can be rung up by the doctor.   118. Will those books be read by the lady?   119. John is being followed everywhere by gangsters.   120. The clock can't be seen from here (by me.)   121. A dress has just been bought in London (by me.)   122. I am being taught to swim (by him.)   123. His homework will have been finished at 9 o'clock (by him.)   124. My dinner was eaten very quickly (by me.)   125. While the dog was being fed in the kitchen (by me), a mouse was caught in the garden by the cat.   126. The books had been corrected very carefully by the teacher.   127. We were taken to the zoo last week by father.   128. Television is watched every evening (by many people.)   129. We will be told the reason soon (by them.)   130. He was allowed three minutes to get ready (by her.)   131. I have never been taught how to ride a bicycle (by anyone.)   132. The money must be paid by the end of the month (by you.)   133. The cakes should be fetched before the shops close (by you.)   134. The house must be painted in the summer (by him.)   135. The letter should have been written yesterday (by you.)   136. The medicine must be taken every three hours (by you.)   137. Tickets should be bought before you get on the tram (by you.)   138. Tickets can no longer be bought from the driver (by you.)   139. If the dog's tail had been pulled (by me), I would have been bitten (by it.)   140. A broken walking-stick was found near his body (by them.)   141. The policeman was taken to Mr. Brown's

Passive

house (by that man).   142. Some burnt papers had also been found there (by them).   143. The man couldn't be caught for a long time (by them).   144. Janet is given a pen by the teacher. A pen is given to Janet by the teacher.   145. I was offered a cup of tea by Aunt Jane. A cup of tea was offered to me by Aunt Jane.   146. Thousands of dolls were sold to the visitors (by the shops).   147. They have just been taught a song by the teacher. A song has just been taught to them by the teacher.   148. The girls were told a nice story by father. A nice story was told to the girls by father.   149. They were shown the rooms (by the owner). The rooms were shown to them (by the owner).   150. Many letters were written to the German girls (by the English girls).   151. I was shown a nice picture by father. A nice picture was shown to me by father.   152. I have just been given a book by mother. A book has just been given to me by mother.   153. I have just been given the book I asked for (by him). The book I asked for has just been given to me (by him).   154. He will be shown pictures by the little girl. Pictures will be shown to him by the little girl.   155. The children were told a nice story (by me). A nice story was told to the children (by me).   156. I was shown my room (by the woman). My room was shown to me (by the woman).   157. They are always given presents (by us). Presents are always given to them (by us).   158. Mary has been sold new shoes by Linda and me. New shoes have been sold to Mary by Linda and me.   159. Their mothers were written a letter by Dick and Hank. A letter was written to their mothers by Dick and Hank.   160. You would be brought the books by father. The books would be brought to you by father.   161. Their brothers were sung a song by John and Tom. A song was sung to their brothers by John and Tom.   162. Father has been given many books by Tina and me. Many books have been given to father by Tina and me.   163. John has been thrown three balls by Tom and me. Three balls have been thrown to John by Tom and me.   164. Their dogs were fed a bone by Ken and Dave. A bone was fed to their dogs by Ken and Dave.   165. Tom has been thrown a ball (by the boys). A ball has been thrown to Tom (by the boys).   166. Our mother is always shown the books (by Linda and me). The books are always shown to our mother (by Linda and me).   167. Their sisters will have been sold some books (by the boys). Some books will have been sold to their sisters (by the boys).   168. Jane is being given new records by Dick. New records are being given to Jane by Dick.   169. Were the girls told the story (by the woman)? Was the story told to the girls (by the woman)?   170. His father was shown many pictures (by the little boy). Many pictures were shown to his father (by the little boy).   171. The ball was thrown to Mary by Tom.   172. The house was being shown to the new guest (by mother).   173. It will be given to you later by Sally.   174. She was given a prize (by them). A prize was given to her (by them).   175. Were you offered a job (by them)? Was a job offered to you (by them)?   176. All the money has been given to the workers (by them).   177. Were you shown all the rooms (by them)? Were all the rooms shown to you (by them)?   178. He has been offered a cup of tea (by them). A cup of tea has been offered to him (by them).   179. John was promised a new car for his birthday (by them). A new car was promised to John for his birthday

Passive

(by them). 180. Were you given enough money (by them)? Was enough money given to you (by them)? 181. I was lent that book for the weekend (by someone). That book was lent to me for the weekend (by someone). 182. Many people have read that book. 183. What will you (they) give the child? 184. Father and mother blew the toy up. 185. Does the man always hold the dogs? 186. Did the thieves steal the car? 187. Bad students will win no prizes. 188. Lions often eat this meat. 189. Such men have often said silly things. 190. She said that a young lady would sing a German song. 191. The good king had made all the people happy. 192. Those men have never made bad mistakes. 193. Tom will bring the gifts for our friends. 194. The boys found the missing bag. 195. They (You) are preparing the meal now. 196. Two men were carrying the suitcases. 197. They will soon forgive you. 198. People (They, You) no longer sell such things. 199. They (You) will give us a lesson tomorrow. 200. They gave her a prize. 201. Did they offer you a job? 202. They gave all the money to the workers. 203. Did they show you all the rooms? 204. They have never taught students how to do that. 205. They (You) sold the house for six thousand pounds. 206. They will arrest him soon. 207. Where do you (they) keep the sugar? 208. The trees hid the house. 209. Did the child break the toy? 210. Does that class often sing those songs? 211. Where will they (you) take the bad man? 212. Those men have sold my sister books. 213. The silly men laughed at many songs. 214. My father looked after the house. 215. Does my sister often catch the balls? 216. Did my sister write the letter? 217. Many people have driven that car. 218. When will they feed the lions? 219. Do they (you) sing that song every Sunday? 220. That girl often wears those two dresses. 221. The man would have hit the ball. 222. Two men heard the girl's song. 223. Boys have often seen the pigs. 224. We (You, People, They) always eat the apples right away. 225. The bad boy beat the dogs. 226. With what does the woman sweep the floors? 227. When did the girl sew the dresses? 228. How many hands am I holding? 229. They have dug a big hole quickly. 230. Father will bring the newspaper upstairs. 231. Workmen still find old bombs every year. 232. How do thieves steal money? 233. The man was lighting the candles when I left. 234. The car has broken the balls. 235. Why did he show you the rooms? 236. How often does their father shake the children? 237. That city is building skyscrapers every year. 238. How many slices of bread has he eaten tonight? 239. Is the owner riding the horse at the moment? 240. The boy was choosing his words carefully. 241. Yes, they will meet us at the station. 242. The dogs would have bitten the girls if they had come near. 243. How long have the thieves hidden the money? 244. You would cut your finger soon if you kept on. 245. When will they give you the prizes? 246. Where did the hunter shoot the deer? 247. The wind will have blown the leaves tomorrow. 248. The little girl fed the birds. 249. The teacher could hear their voices if they spoke louder. 250. That player had caught eight balls.

Reported Speech

15. Reported Speech

1. He said that he had gone home at 2 o'clock the previous day (the day before).   2. He said that he would go home. . .   3. He said that he always went . . 4. He said that he had been going home . . .   5. He said that he wanted to go . . .   6. He said that he had wanted to go . . .   7. He said that he had to go . . .   8. He said that he had had to go . . .   9. He said that he would have to go . . .   10. He said that he had to go . . .   11. He said that he would be going . . .   12. Peter asked Jim if he would send it back the next day (the day after, the following day).   13. John said to Jane that she had forgotten to send him a present.   14. John asked George if his dog bit.   15. Jim said to Dave that he should take . . .   16. John told Jim not to tell Mary.   17. Tom said that his brother had gone home.   18. Mary asked Dick if he was laughing at her.   19. Jim asked Linda to go with him.   20. Bill asked Harry how much he had paid for his coat.   21. Mary told Bill to find her a nice book.   22. Ann told Jim that that piece of cake was for him.   23. Fred told Helen that she had put her umbrella in his car the previous day (the day before).   24. Father told Mother to give Jim . . .   25. Father told Mother that he would see Jim the following day (the next day; the day after).   26. Mary asked Bill if he had heard the . . .   27. Mary asked Bill to open the window.   28. Fred said that he was going to the city that day and that he would fly to London in two days time (two days after; two days later).   29. Mary asked Jim where he had hidden her shoe.   30. Bill asked Ann how long they had known each other.   31. The man told the girl that he would ring her father up if he caught her there again.   32. Jim said to Tom that he had seen him there two years before.   33. Mary asked Father if he had bought the books up to that time.   34. Linda said that she would be going to school the next year (the following year; the year after).   35. Jim told Mary to talk louder. / Jim asked Mary to talk louder.   36. John said that his sister had flown to New York the previous week (the week before).   37. Mary asked if they would come . . .   38. Mary asked if they should be there . . .   39. Father told Bill that he couldn't have a car.   40. Mother told Linda that she was sorry that she couldn't help her . . .   41. The thief warned the boy that he would kill him if he shouted.   42. Your father promised us that he would go to the zoo with us.   43. Bill maintained that he wanted to marry Betty.   44. Sue responded that she had known them when they had been young.   45. Tom and Lucy proudly said that they had done everything themselves.   46. The Taylors complained that they had had a . . .   47. Dotty asked us if we had been at . . .   48. The men asked their wives if they had really gone there the previous night (the night before).   49. Peter said that he promised to be . . .   50. The girl asked me if I would help her the following day (the next day; the day after).   51. She asked him if he had read the newspaper the previous day (the day before).   52. They said to us that we should walk slowly if we didn't want to fall.   53. He told us to look at the shops and not to talk so loudly.   54. She said that she had bought that dress two days before (two days earlier).   55. He asked her if she saw . . .   56. She asked him if he was flying to Moscow the following

day (the next day; the day after).   57. He said that he had read 20 books that year and that the previous year (the year before) he had read only 15 but that the next year (the following year; the year after) he would certainly read more. 58. The boy told the policeman that he couldn't see them then (at that time). 59. She said to the boy that she had cleaned the kitchen twice that day. If he thought that she was going to clean it again because he had broken the dish, then he was wrong. She would wait until the next day (the following day; the day after). 60. Mary said that she was going to the cinema the next day (the following day; the day after).   61. Mary told Jim that he could have dinner with them that evening.   62. Mary said that they would go to the beach when they had had lunch. 63. Mary said that she didn't like cats but that she liked dogs.   64. Mary told Jim to come quickly and to see what she had done.   65. Mary asked Jim when they would arrive.   66. Mary said that she hadn't finished her homework the previous day (the day before) because she had been so tired after the party two days earlier (two days before).   67. Mary said that her aunt lived in that house over there. 68. Mary said to Jim that he should close the window before he left.   69. Mary said that Jim had to hand in his book and then he could go home.   70. Mary asked her mother at what time the party would start.   71. John said to Paul that they could see the rabbits if they walked quietly.   72. Mary said that she had been at the cinema the previous day (the day before) and that she had to visit her grandmother the following day (the next day; the day after).   73. She said that Susan would be in Bonn that afternoon.   74. My boss asked me if I was going home . . .   75. They told us that they would be playing cards after they had had lunch.   76. Father told Mike to wipe his shoes before he came in.   77. The woman asked us why we hadn't washed the cups.   78. Mary said that she hadn't seen anyone there two hours before.   79. I said that Mary and Peter were coming that day and that Bill was not leaving until the next (the following) Wednesday (the Wednesday after).   80. Aunt Jane said to Peter that he should switch the light off and close the door before he left . . .   81. We asked the stewardess when the plane arrived . . .   82. The policeman asked the boy what his name was. 83. You said to us that we should take our coats . . .   84. You said to us that we had held . . . 85. He said that he had to go . . .   86. The doctor asked the man if his toe hurt.   87. Father asked us how far we were walking that day. 88. The woman said that she would play . . .   89. The doctor asked Marie why she hadn't taken her baby to the hospital the previous week (the week before). 90. The teacher told us to leave the building.   91. Mother said to you that you had done . . .   92. The men asked the girls if they had gone there the previous day (the day before).   93. Martha said to me that I should not work . . . 94. The old woman said that her sister had lived there two years before.   95. The captain said to his men that they couldn't leave if the weather didn't change.   96. He said that he would come as soon as he had finished the book he was reading. 97. Mrs. Jones said that she would help him if she could.   98. Their daughter said to them that she was not going to school that day.   99. Her mother asked us why we hadn't tried . . .   100. He asked her if she could come. 101. He said

Reported Speech

to us that we should get out of his house . . . 102. She asked him if he wanted . . . 103. My mother asked me if I was washing my face. 104. John told us that someone had broken into his house the previous night (the night before). 105. Jane said to us that she was glad to hear that we were so . . . 106. She told her to have . . . 107. Linda told Dave (said to Dave) that they hadn't seen . . . 108. Dave asked Linda what she had been doing. 109. I said to her that I had something to show her. 110. She said that nothing ever grew in her . . . 111. He said to his mother that he was going away the next day (the following day; the day after). 112. They said that they had a lift but that it very often didn't work. 113. The small boy said that he had an English lesson the following day (the next day; the day after) and that he hadn't done his homework up to that time. 114. The boy said that he was going fishing with his father that . . . 115. Mrs. Small said that she would wait until her boy came in but she hoped that he wouldn't be . . . 116. The policeman asked the man what his name was. 117. The boys asked the girls if they had come there the previous day (the day before). 118. Mother told him to look . . . 119. You said to us that we should take our dogs for a walk at that time (then). 120. They said to her that she had written . . . 121. You asked me when I would come home the following day (the next day; the day after). 122. She told us that we would see two dogs if we went there. 123. He said to you that you would have seen the word if you had read . . . 124. You said that he hadn't eaten the apple after he had stolen it. 125. He said to me that I could go to the zoo with him in two days time (two days after; two days later) if I was helping my mother then (at that time). 126. He asked his wife if she wanted him to come . . . 127. He said that he promised that he would be home . . . 128. Judy told Bill that she would miss him . . . 129. Fred told Helen that he had lost his key but that he had found hers. 130. George said that he thought that he had left it on his desk. 131. He explained that he had missed . . . 132. John asked Mary what she was doing. 133. John asked Peter how the film had ended. 134. George asked Mary why his food wasn't ready. 135. The waitress asked the lady if she would like tea. 136. Tom asked Jane if she could catch . . . 137. We answered that he was sitting over there. 138. Ruth told Ken not to drink . . . /Ruth said to Ken that he shouldn't drink. . . /Ruth ordered Ken not to drink . . . 139. They asked us if we hadn't bought a tree up to that time. 140. They said that he had sat there for two hours at that time (then). 141. Linda asked them where they would sleep the following day (the day after; the next day). 142. Tom said to Peggy that he would forget the words again if she taught (had taught) him the words that day. 143. He said that he spent all his money . . . 144. Bob said to Dolly that she should hold his book. / Bob told Dolly to hold his book. 145. They said to us that we had thrown the chair away three years before. 146. She said to me that she would not say that if she were (was) me. 147. She said that she swam . . . 148. Linda said to Bob that she had to show him the book the following day (the next day; the day after). 149. They said to us that we had sat there two days before. 150. Linda said that then (at that time) the men had shot five birds there that afternoon. 151. They told me that I had not sat there

Reported Speech

the day before (the previous day).   152. We said that we would not bring you there . . .   153. Tom said to Becky that he would not go with her if it weren't (hadn't been) . . . 154. Bill said that he was learning . . .   155. Ben said to Linda that she would see Carter if she flew to New York in two days time (two days later; two days after).   156. She said that she knew all the people there.   157. Tom asked them when they would go the following year (the year after; the next year).   158. They said that he had been wearing a brown coat the previous day (the day before). 159. Ruth told Mac to sing . . .   160. Tom told Linda not to drive . . . /Tom said to Linda that she shouldn't drive . . . /Tom ordered Linda not to drive . . . 161. They said that he had been feeding the deer the previous day (the day before). 162. Ben asked Peggy when she had ridden . . .   163. Linda said that she had cut her finger two days earlier (two days before).   164. Mother told Father that she would not ask him to go if she could go.   165. Mom said that they had found ten toys unter the chairs there at that time (then).   166. She said that she loved her new . . .   167. John said to Linda that she should take . . .   168. Linda said that she had to sell her books in two days time (two days later; two days after). 169. Linda told Tom not to blow . . .   170. Jenny told her boyfriend that she hadn't kept his ring.   171. The man said to his sister that he had bought two dresses for her that week.   172. Richard asked his mother what she had done two weeks before.   173. Bob said to Susan that she shouldn't begin to read.   174. My brother asked Linda if she always threw her books . . .   175. Tom reported that he wouldn't go . . .   176. Bob said to Linda that he had known her . . . 177. Susan told Jenny to buy tomatoes that day. 178. Linda said to me that she would hold my book there. 179. The boys asked us if we had sold our car. 180. Cathy replied that she was drinking milk then (at that time). 181. Tom asked Peggy to give him her pen.   182. Carl told Susan that she hadn't thought of that the previous day (the day before).   183. The woman told her husband that she would be singing that song two days later (in two days time; two days after). 184. Tom said to Peggy that she should catch that ball.   185. Daniel said that he often took. . .   186. The girls said to their mothers that they had been running to school when they had seen them.   187. My sister asked me when I would wake up the following day (the day after; the next day).   188. Cathy told Ben that she didn't understand what he had said.   189. Mary asked Peter at what time he got up.   190. The mother told her girl that she could go to school when she was . . .   191. Tom said that he had visited the British Museum while he had been on holiday that year.   192. Mother told us to hurry up or we would be late. . . 193. The girl told me that I would have to take the dog out every day if I had a dog.   194. The girl asked her boyfriend why he hadn't stayed at home the previous night (the night before).   195. The doctor said to Miss Smith that he thought that he had seen her before.   196. The teacher said to us that we should open our books and (should) begin . . .   197. Jim told Linda that he hadn't seen anyone there two hours before.   198. The man asked his daughter if she had seen his pen.   199. The lady asked me if I liked . . . 200. Bill told Mary that she had left her umbrella in his car the previous day (the day before).   201. The man

Reported Speech

asked the children if they had been to the zoo that week. 202. Mary said that she had seen the car accident but she denied that she had caused it. 203. The children asked if they could take . . . 204. Peggy asked Tom if he was coming to her party the next day (the following day; the day after). 205. Dan asked Linda if she had told his sister . . . 206. The boys asked their father if they had to go to the doctor's the next day (the following day; the day after). 207. Judy said to Tom that she had gone there earlier than he. 208. Linda said that she would go . . . 209. Dan said that he had heard . . . 210. Tom said to his mother that they went . . . 211. Andrea said that they had seen . . . 212. Ann said that Linda and she had thrown her ball two days before. 213. Susan said to father that he would buy a car the following week (the week after; the next week). 214. Tom said to Jane that he was sure that he had left her book on his desk. 215. Father warned the girls not to stay too long or they would have to go. . . 216. The teacher told us that we wouldn't understand what he (she) was (had been) saying if we didn't work . . . 217. Mary reported that she had been at home the previous day (the day before) and that she was going to the zoo the next day (the following day; the day after). 218. John replied that he had visited his uncle three weeks before. 219. She said to father that she was leaving the next day (the following day; the day after). 220. Linda told Dick that she would be with him as soon as she was ready. 221. Dan explained that they would go . . . 222. The teacher told the children that they had played very much that day. 223. They shouted that he was washing . . . 224. Father said to Linda that she couldn't go . . . 225. Tom's sister replied that he always came . . . 226. The boys said that they would be taking the test the following day (the next day; the day after). 227. Their father said to the girls that they had gone to church the previous day (the day before). 228. The neighbour said to Tom that he had seen him often. 229. The teacher said that the boy would be going . . . 230. She replied that she had been there . . . 231. They said to Tom that they didn't want to see him then (at that time). 232. The daughter answered that she had come home that day. 233. Tom said to Betty that he wanted to marry her. 234. Mother said to Linda that she hadn't played . . . 235. d.) 236. d.) 237. d.) 238. a.) 239. b.) 240. a.) 241. d.) 242. d.) 243. b.) 244. a.) 245. c.) 246. b.) 247. b.) 248. a.) 249. a.) 250. b.) 251. c.) 252. c.) 253. d.) 254. b.) 255. b.) 256. a.) 257. c

16. Some — any

1. some 2. anything 3. some 4. any 5. some 6. Something 7. some
8. anywhere 9. any 10. some 11. anything 12. Some 13. any
14. some 15. Some 16. any 17. some 18. somewhere 19. some
20. some 21. anything 22. Somebody 23. any 24. some 25. anything
26. some 27. any 28. some 29. anybody 30. something
31. somewhere 32. anywhere 33. some; some 34. any 35. some
36. any 37. somewhere 38. some 39. something 40. anywhere
41. some 42. anybody 43. Somebody 44. some 45. some 46. any
47. Something 48. anybody 49. Some 50. any 51. something
52. some 53. anywhere 54. anybody 55. some 56. any
57. somewhere 58. any 59. some 60. any 61. anywhere 62. some
63. Somebody 64. anything 65. some 66. anybody 67. some
68. Something 69. some 70. any 71. Somebody 72. any 73. some
74. some 75. somebody 76. any 77. something 78. some
79. anywhere 80. anybody 81. some 82. anything 83. some
84. anything 85. some 86. some 87. anybody 88. somewhere
89. anywhere 90. some 91. some 92. Somebody 93. any 94. Some
95. somewhere 96. anything 97. any 98. somewhere 99. some
100. anywhere 101. something 102. anybody

17. Adverbials

1. excited; fast   2. kind   3. hastily   4. polite; attentively   5. angrily   6. well   7. beautiful; quickly   8. noisy   9. slowly   10. nice   11. quickly   12. slowly; angry   13. fast; fast   14. hard; patiently   15. curious; eagerly   16. good; well   17. loudly   18. excellent; proudly; unusual   19. attentive; distinctly   20. excitedly   21. nervous; quickly   22. curious   23. courageous; curiously   24. excited   25. carelessly   26. quickly   27. happy; nicely   28. kind   29. kindly   30. easily   31. slow; slowly   32. angry; angrily   33. slowly; slow   34. beautiful; beautifully   35. bad; badly   36. punctual; punctually   37. good; well   38. fast; fast   39. careful; carefully   40. quickly; quickly   41. good   42. properly   43. kind   44. polite; polite   45. politely   46. good   47. excited   48. exciting   49. excited; exciting   50. attentive; attentively   51. angrily; angry   52. kind; kindly   53. nice; nicely   54. slowly; slow   55. poor; poorly   56. happily; happy   57. fast   58. angry; quickly   59. careful; hard; noisily   60. excited; tidily; neatly   61. distinctly; well   62. well   63. hard; quickly   64. pretty; happily   65. fast   66. sweet; beautifully   67. angrily   68. hard   69. fast; slowly   70. She has often been here.   71. We never go for a walk.   72. They never take a walk before breakfast. / Before breakfast they never take a walk.   73. We went to the shop yesterday. / Yesterday we went to the shop.   74. My father never works hard at home. / At home my father never works hard.   75. The young man often swims in the morning. / In the morning the young man often swims.   76. She will ride a bicycle to the shop carefully. / She will carefully ride a bicycle to the shop.   77. Ben has seldom read a book.   78. Today you have sung three songs in your room. / You have sung three songs in your room today.   79. We never find our books on the table.   80. She always comes to Cologne at 12 o'clock. / At 12 o'clock she always comes to Cologne.   81. Yesterday they went to the zoo quietly. / Yesterday they quietly went to the zoo. / They went to the zoo quietly yesterday. / They quietly went to the zoo yesterday. / They went to the zoo yesterday quietly.   82. Tomorrow I will open the door noisily. / I will open the door noisily tomorrow. / I will noisily open the door tomorrow. / Tomorrow I will noisily open the door.   83. Last year you seldom helped us. / You seldom helped us last year.   84. We saw them in the kitchen this morning. / This morning we saw them in the kitchen.   85. The old lady seldom goes out in the evening. / In the evening the old lady seldom goes out.   86. She always goes for a swim after school. / After school she always goes for a swim.   87. I shall run to the doctor quickly. / I shall quickly run to the doctor.   88. She arrived at the station yesterday. / Yesterday she arrived at the station.   89. She has often forgotten things.   90. I have seen her at the circus this afternoon. / This afternoon I have seen her at the circus.   91. At the office she works busily. / She busily works at the office. / She works at the office busily.   92. I must go to bed at 8 o'clock. / At 8 o'clock I must go to bed.   93. We shall visit you next week. / Next week we shall visit you.   94. Mike always eats chocolate during the lessons. / During the lessons Mike always eats chocolate.   95. They always go shopping

Adverbials

on Saturdays. / On Saturdays they always go shopping.   96. They often buy sweets at the supermarket. / At the supermarket they often buy sweets.   97. Mr. Potter quickly finished his meal. / Mr. Potter finished his meal quickly.   98. The old woman climbed the stairs slowly. / The old woman slowly climbed the stairs.   99. The boys went for a swim in the sea before lunch. / Before lunch the boys went for a swim in the sea.   100. At 8 o'clock they have breakfast in the kitchen. / They have breakfast in the kitchen at 8 o'clock.   101. We always spend our holidays in London. / In London we always spend our holidays.   102. We carefully planned our holidays. / We planned our holidays carefully.   103. She often sunbathed on the beach. / On the beach she often sunbathed.   104. Tim carefully closed the window. / Tim closed the window carefully.   105. I was at home yesterday. / Yesterday I was at home.   106. We saw her in the bus this morning. / This morning we saw her in the bus.   107. She did her homework carefully. / She carefully did her homework.   108. We shall arrive punctually. / We shall punctually arrive.   109. I quickly ran to the bus stop. / I ran to the bus stop quickly.   110. They always went to school at 8 o'clock. / At 8 o'clock they always went to school.   111. She never talked to me angrily in the morning. / In the morning she never talked to me angrily. / She never talked to me in the morning angrily.   112. We have often sung a song noisily in the bathroom. / We have often sung a song in the bathroom noisily. / In the bathroom we have often sung a song noisily.   113. He never got up at 5 o'clock. / At 5 o'clock he never got up.   114. The lady sat in the sun every day. / Every day the lady sat in the sun.   115. The men always sang songs happily at church. / At church the men always sang songs happily. / The men always sang songs at church happily.   116. The children clapped their hands loudly during the show. / The children loudly clapped their hands during the show. / The children clapped their hands during the show loudly. / During the show the children clapped their hands loudly. / During the show the children loudly clapped their hands.   117. We usually wash our faces quickly in the bathroom in the morning. / In the morning we usually wash our faces quickly in the bathroom. / In the morning we usually wash our faces in the bathroom quickly.   118. We will always take the dog for a walk before school. / Before school we will always take the dog for a walk.   119. By tomorrow the children will have seen the kittens three times. / The children will have seen the kittens three times by tomorrow.   120. The boys were happily eating apples in their room in the afternoon. / The boys were eating apples in their room happily in the afternoon. / In the afternoon the boys were happily eating apples in their room. / In the afternoon the boys were eating apples happily in their room. / In the afternoon the boys were eating apples in their room happily.   121. I would never have gone to that house at night. / At night I would never have gone to that house.   122. My sister had sometimes cleaned her room fast on Saturday. / On Saturday my sister had sometimes cleaned her room fast.

18. Reflexive Pronouns

1. herself 2. ourselves 3. herself 4. yourselves 5. each other 6. ourselves 7. themselves 8. yourself 9. myself 10. herself 11. themselves 12. myself 13. herself 14. myself 15. ourselves 16. himself 17. ourselves 18. herself 19. yourselves 20. ourselves 21. yourself 22. herself 23. himself 24. ourselves 25. myself 26. themselves 27. yourself 28. themselves 29. myself 30. yourselves 31. yourself 32. each other 33. himself 34. herself 35. myself 36. myself 37. yourselves 38. themselves 39. myself 40. themselves 41. herself 42. myself 43. himself 44. myself 45. themselves 46. myself 47. herself 48. yourself 49. each other 50. himself 51. myself 52. herself 53. yourself/yourselves 54. herself 55. itself 56. himself 57. ourselves 58. themselves; each other 59. — 60. — 61. I settled myself down. . . 62. — 63. We prepared ourselves. . . 64. — 65. The dog proved itself. . . 66. — 67. — 68. The girls dressed themselves. . . 69. — 70. They settled themselves. . . 71. — 72. — 73. Did you shave yourself. . . 74. I hurt my hand myself. 75. — 76. Did the children behave themselves? 77. I cut my finger myself. 78. — 79. The girls dressed themselves. 80. The little children enjoyed themselves very much. 81. The children were ashamed of themselves. 82. We had to wash ourselves quickly. 83. The children hid themselves. 84. The girl talked to herself. 85. Did you hurt yourself? 86. The courageous children asserted themselves. 87. The boy cut himself. 88. Behave yourself! 89. Does the boy have to shave himself already? 90. Did you sew it yourself? 91. Can I make myself useful? 92. Did you want to do it yourself? 93. The ladies introduced themselves. 94. They looked at themselves in the mirror. 95. I seated myself. 96. Help yourself to a piece of cake. 97. The boy and the girl fell in love. 98. We saw each other through the window. 99. I wanted to look at the city by myself. 100. I introduced the ladies. 101. You should help each other. 102. The crying mothers had to pull themselves together. 103. Did his wife support herself or her husband? 104. The boy hurt himself. 105. The girl traveled all by herself. 106. We thought of each other constantly.

19. Future

1. does the show start   2. arrives   3. starts   4. start   5. end   6. begin   7. must you take / do you have to take   8. does the train leave   9. you are going shopping   10. is getting   11. Are you going   12. he is doing   13. am taking   14. is John taking a walk   15. is your child starting   16. am going   17. is father working   18. are you doing   19. are your guests coming   20. are driving   21. am planning to wash   22. are you going   23. Will you be   24. will certainly snow   25. will go   26. Will we see   27. will dry   28. will you take   29. will bake   30. will we do   31. will father be   32. will cry   33. will you cook   34. will have   35. will you wear   36. will get married   37. will eat   38. will/shall be landing   39. will be starting   40. will/shall probably be sleeping   41. will be sleeping   42. will be coming   43. will be reading   44. will be wearing   45. will be working   46. will be arriving   47. will be going   48. will be going   49. will be going   50. will/shall be seeing   51. will be raining   52. will be arriving   53. Is he going to meet   54. are you going to tell   55. Are you going to play   56. is going to rain   57. is going to get married   58. are they going to visit   59. aren't we going to take   60. Is your brother going to wash   61. Are the men going to stop work   62. am going to have   63. Is your sister going to drive   64. are you going to be   65. Isn't your friend going to phone   66. are you going to study   67. are going to buy   68. will all be taking / are all taking   69. is going to have to take / will have to take   70. Will church start / Will church be starting / Does church start   71. will get   72. will be walking   73. Is he flying / Is he going to fly   74. won't be dying / won't die   75. are going to take   76. are going to take   77. will grow up   78. are going to have / will have   79. does the queen arrive   80. is staying / will stay / is going to stay / will be staying   81. I will/shall help you this evening.   82. The marriage/wedding will be taking place in June.   83. War is going to come.   84. You train leaves at 8 o'clock this coming Tuesday.   85. When are you going to church tomorrow?   86. I am taking the test/examination this coming Wednesday.   87. We will be landing on the moon in ten years.   88. My brother will show the people how they must drive.   89. The baby thinks its mother is going to feed it.   90. In America the Fourth of July celebration starts at 9 p. m.   91. We will be sleeping longer tomorrow.   92. Will you phone us when you have arrived home?   93. Dan is driving/traveling to Bonn on Friday.   94. The cat hopes that the mouse is going to come out of the hole.   95. We will be getting married tomorrow./ We are getting married tomorrow.   96. a.   97. a./b.   98. b.   99. a./b.   100. a.   101. a./b.   102. b.   103. a.   104. b.   105. a./b.   106. a./b.   107. a.   108. b.   109. a.   110. a./b.   111. b.   112. a.   113. b.   114. a./b.   115. a./b.   116. a.

Auxiliaries

20. Auxiliaries

1. can kill / is able to kill   2. can walk / is able to walk   3. could work / was able to work   4. will not be able to see   5. can see / are able to see   6. has been able to talk   7. would be able to play   8. Have you been able to talk   9. Will you be able to watch   10. may come / might come   11. might have come / may have come   12. may be / might be   13. may have seen / might have seen   14. might eat   15. might have done   16. may have read / might have read   17. may go / can go / are allowed to go / are permitted to go   18. may (not) go / can (not) go / were (not) allowed to go / were (not) permitted to go / were forbidden to go   19. may go / can go / will be permitted to go / will be allowed to go   20. Are you always allowed to go / Are you always permitted to go   21. May I smoke? / Can I smoke? / Am I allowed to smoke? / Am I permitted to smoke?   22. Has he really not been allowed to read / Has he really not been permitted to read   23. may not drink / can not drink / are not allowed to drink / are not permitted to drink / are forbidden to drink   24. Have they never been allowed to paint / Have they never been permitted to paint   25. have never been allowed to do / have never been permitted to do / have been forbidden to do   26. Would he be allowed to see / Would he be permitted to see   27. have to do / must do   28. have to do / must do   29. was forced to go / was compelled to go   30. will have to leave / will be forced to leave / will be compelled to leave   31. have often had to run / have often been forced to run / have often been compelled to run   32. would have had to shoot / would have been forced to shoot / would have been compelled to shoot   33. have had to work / have been forced to work / have been compelled to work   34. was forced to go / was compelled to go / had to go   35. will have to brush / will be forced to brush / will be compelled to brush   36. had had to eat / had been forced to eat / had been compelled to eat   37. need not get up / will not be forced to get up / will not be compelled to get up / will not have to get up   38. would have had to go / would have been forced to go / would have been compelled to go   39. should have come / ought to have come / was to have come / was expected to have come / was supposed to have come   40. should help / ought to help / will be expected to help / will be supposed to help / will have to help   41. would be expected to go / would be supposed to go / would have to go   42. should do / ought to do / are to do / are expected to do / are supposed to do / have to do   43. was to arrive / was expected to arrive / was supposed to arrive   44. have always been expected to comb / have always been supposed to comb / have always had to comb   45. would not have been expected to help / would not have been supposed to help / would not have had to help   46. had been expected to go / should have gone / ought to have gone / was to have gone / was expected to have gone / was supposed to have gone   47. would be expected to wash / would be supposed to wash / would have to wash   48. will be expected to take / will be supposed to take / will have to take / should take / ought to take   49. need not bring / don't have to bring   50. is no need to bring / isn't any need to bring   51. was not necessary to bring / is not necessary to bring

Auxiliaries

52. need not come / don't have to come   53. would be necessary to come   54. would have been no need to come / wouldn't have been any need to come   55. can 56. need not   57. must   58. must   59. should / ought to   60. must not   61. may / can   62. must not   63. should / ought to   64. must   65. must not   66. need not   67. must   68. must not   69. need not   70. may / might   71. must   72. should / ought to   73. must not   74. must   75. must   76. should / ought to   77. may / might   78. need not   79. may / can   80. will not be necessary   81. was not allowed to / was forbidden to / was not permitted to   82. Have you never been expected to / Have you never been supposed to / Have you never had to   83. Would they be able to   84. will have to / will be forced to / will be compelled to   85. would have been no necessity to / wouldn't have been any necessity to   86. Have you been allowed to / Have you been permitted to   87. is their duty   88. did not have to   89. will have to / will be forced to / will be compelled to   90. Would they be able to   91. have to   92. have had to / have been expected to / have been supposed to   93. is his duty   94. did not have to   95. Would you be able to   96. will have to / will be forced to / will be compelled to   97. Have they ever been expected to / Have they ever been supposed to / Have they ever had to   98. is your duty to   99. have never had to / have never been expected to / have never been supposed to   100. will have to / will be forced to / will be compelled to   101. would have been no necessity to / wouldn't have been any necessity to   102. has to   103. were forbidden to   104. Would he be able to   105. a/c   106. c   107. a/b   108. a/c   109. a   110. b/c   111. a/c   112. possibility   113. obligation   114. necessity   115. compulsion   116. permission   117. ability   118. obligation   119. necessity; compulsion   120. prohibition   121. possibility   122. necessity; compulsion   123. possibility   124. obligation   125. compulsion   126. permission   127. necessity   128. necessity   129. ability   130. I will be able to help you now.   131. We have not had to now.   131. We have not had to wash the curtains every week.   132. The baby will really have to go to bed now.   133. Father said I will not be allowed to go (will not be permitted to go; will be forbidden to go) swimming tomorrow.   134. We weren't to drink so much water. / We weren't supposed to drink so much water. 135. We will have to be going now.   136. You were to wash the dishes. / You were supposed to wash the dishes.   137. The children won't have to be so quiet. 138. Has he been able to walk without help?   139. The plane will have to be arriving any minute.   140. You were not allowed to touch the pictures! / You were forbidden to touch the pictures! / You were not permitted to touch the pictures! 141. We won't be able to see the sun at night.   142. I have been forced to do my homework every day. / I have been compelled to do my homework every day. / I have had to do my homework every day.   143. Won't you be able to write your name?   144. You were to go to bed. / You were supposed to go to bed. 145. Would Tom be permitted to go with us? / Would Tom be allowed to go with us?   146. could not walk / was not able to walk.   147. may go / might go 148. will have to do / will be forced to do / will be compelled to do   149. need not buy / do not have to buy   150. could (not) / were (not)

Auxiliaries

able to   151. shouldn't / ought not to / aren't supposed to   152. ought not   153. need not / don't have to   154. were allowed to / were permitted to   155. will have to / will be forced to / will be compelled to / will be expected to / will be supposed to   156. had / were forced   157. may have gone / might have gone   158. would not have had to go / would not have been forced to go / would not have been compelled to go 159. should / ought to / are to / (are to be doing) / are expected to / (are expected to be doing) / are supposed to (are supposed to be doing)   160. had to / was forced to / was compelled to   161. will not be allowed to go / will not be permitted to go / will be forbidden to go / are not allowed to go / are not permitted to go / are forbidden to go / may not go / cannot go   162. will have to / must / will be forced to / will be compelled to   163. need not / doesn't have to.   164. might be   165. will you have to go / will you be forced to go / will you be compelled to go   166. could hardly understand / was hardly able to understand   167. must wear / have to wear   168. was never allowed to go / was never permitted to go   169. would not have to paint   170. could have helped / would have been able to help; couldn't help / wasn't able to help   171. may / can / are allowed to / are permitted to   172. must not / are forbidden to / are not allowed to / are not permitted to / may not   173. could not / was not able to   174. Can / Are you able to; cannot / am not able to; can / will be able to   175. had to / was forced to / was compelled to   176. must / has to; need not / does not have to   177. cannot / is not able to; will be able to   178. was allowed to / was permitted to / could   179. May / Can / Am I allowed to / Am I permitted to; may not / cannot / are not allowed to / are not permitted to / are forbidden to; will be allowed to / will be permitted to   180. don't have to / need not   181. must not / are forbidden to   182. will have to / will be forced to / will be compelled to   183. may / can / are allowed to / are permitted to   184. must / has to; need not / does not have to   185. could not / were not able to; Can / Are you able to   186. should / ought to / are expected to / are supposed to   187. may / might   188. should / ought to / is supposed to / is expected to / is to / has to   189. may have cried / might have cried / may have been crying / might have been crying   190. I can not swim. / I am not able to swim.   191. When I was two years old, I could not swim (I was not able to swim).   192. When I am 80 years old, I will not be able to swim.   193. Until my grandmother died, I could go (was able to go) to her every Sunday.   194. Can you play the piano? / Are you able to play the piano?   195. He has been able to speak for five years.   196. She could already walk (She was already able to walk) when she was one year old.   197. They (You) will be able to drive home in two hours.   198. I may not be here at 5 o'clock.   199. I might not take the airplane.   200. She may have gone earlier.   201. They (You) were afraid that wolves might be in the woods.   202. That might not have happened if she had been here.   203. You may have been in the kitchen.   204. They (You) were afraid that he might not go.   205. She thought that he might be dead.   206. It might rain.   207. May I go? / Can I go? / Am I allowed to go? / Am I permitted to go?   208. You may not smoke in the tram. / You must not smoke in the tram. / You are not allowed to smoke in the tram. /

Auxiliaries

You are not permitted to smoke in the tram. / You are forbidden to smoke in the tram.   209. When I was ten years old, I was allowed to (was permitted to) go to another city alone.   210. You will be allowed to (will be permitted to) get married when you are 18.   211. For the past year I have been allowed to (have been permitted to) go to bed at 10 p. m.   212. If he was 18, he would be allowed to (would be permitted to) vote.   213. We were not allowed to (were not permitted to / were forbidden to) talk too loudly.   214. You did not help me; therefore you may not (cannot / are not permitted to / are not allowed to / are forbidden to) have an ice.   215. Children are not allowed to (are not permitted to / are forbidden to / may not / must not) enter the building site.   216. The passengers were not allowed to (were not permitted to / were forbidden to) leave the airplane.   217. The dress may not be (must not be) washed too often.   218. You may not (cannot / are not allowed to / are not permitted to) go home yet.   219. I must (have to) go shopping.   220. You must (have to / are forced to) go to the doctor's.   221. He had to (was forced to) stay home.   222. He must (will have to / will be forced to) fly to Munich tomorrow.   223. Have you ever had to (Have you ever been forced to / Have you ever been compelled to) eat grass?   224. You need not (don't have to) go yet.   225. Yes, I must (have to / am forced to) go.   226. You should be (ought to be / are to be / are expected to be / are supposed to be / have to be) home at 8 p. m.   227. He should not (ought not to / is not to) speak (talk) so loudly.   228. When she is 18, she has to (will have to / will be expected to) celebrate her birthday.   229. I should not have (ought not to have / was not to have / was not expected to have / was not supposed to have) done that.   230. You should have (ought to have / were to have / were expected to have / were supposed to have) helped us.   231. They (you) were to have (were expected to have / were supposed to have / should have / ought to have) come yesterday.   232. I really should not (ought not to / am not to / am not supposed to) go there.   233. He must (has to) eat in order to live.   234. You don't have to (need not) do that if you don't want to.   235. I didn't have to go (It wasn't necessary for me to go) along yesterday.   236. We won't have to go (It won't be necessary for us to go) by bus if we have a car.   237. She must go (has to go) to the dentist twice a year.   238. He might come tomorrow.   239. You may not (must not / are not allowed to / are not permitted to / are forbidden to) leave the room.   240. He said he could (would be able to) come tomorrow.   241. We need not be (don't have to be / It isn't necessary for us to be) there early.   242. You shouldn't eat (ought not to eat / aren't supposed to eat / aren't to eat) so much.   243. Was he allowed to (Was he permitted to) go swimming yesterday?   244. You must get up (You'll have to get up / You'll be forced to get up / You'll be compelled to get up) early tomorrow.   245. If he came now, would you then be permitted to (would you then be allowed to) go with me?   246. If he had been here, he might have gone with us.   247. I could have helped (I would have been able to help) you if you had told me.   248. When did you have to go (were you forced to go) to bed yesterday?   249. I should have helped (ought to have helped / was to have helped / was expected to have helped) her.   250. What can (may) I write?   251. She was expected to

Auxiliaries

(was supposed to / was to) help.   252. Will you have to (Will you be forced to / Will you be compelled to) read the book?   253. We have been forbidden to smoke here.   254. It won't be necessary to (There won't be any need to / There will be no need to) sell the car.   255. We may drive (travel) tomorrow.   256. We will be able to come tomorrow.   257. He might have written.   258. Would they be allowed to (Would they be permitted to) visit us tomorrow?   259. We might have helped.   260. He will be able to read next year.   261. You should have gone (ought to have gone / were supposed to have gone / were to have gone) to bed earlier.   262. I may be ill (sick) tomorrow.   263. I might have come if you had asked me.   264. When I was ill (sick), I had to stay (was forced to stay / was compelled to stay) in bed.   265. The doctor said I would be allowed to (would be permitted to) get up three days later; then I would be able to eat normally again.   266. Children under 18 years of age are not allowed to (are not permitted to / are forbidden to) drink alcohol.   267. I cannot help (am not able to help) you at the moment because I have to (am supposed to / am to) clean up my room.   268. He said that he could not come (was not able to come) because he had to (was forced to) clean the windows.   269. He should have cleaned (ought to have cleaned / was to have cleaned / was supposed to have cleaned) the windows; but instead of that he went swimming.   270. Do we have to do (Must we do) that; is it really necessary?   271. Why can't you come (Why won't you be able to come) next week?   272. I am not allowed to (I am not permitted to / I am forbidden to) because it is my duty to play with my little brother.   273. Would you be allowed to come (Would you be permitted to come) if my sister played with your brother?   274. Hopefully she will soon be able to go home.   275. Last year she could not (was not able to) speak yet.   276. We may be able to go tomorrow.   277. He might have been allowed (permitted) to go.   278. We may not go (cannot go / are not allowed to go / are forbidden to go / are not permitted to go) there.   279. He was allowed to go (was permitted to go) home yesterday.   280. May we see (Can we see / Are we allowed to see / Are we permitted to see) the child?   281. He will be allowed to (will be permitted to) travel to London next year.   282. As (Because) no tram came, I had to (was forced to / was compelled to) walk.   283. You will have to (will be forced to) stay home tomorrow morning because your mother is ill (sick).   284. They (You) should really have been (ought really to have been / were really expected to have been / were really supposed to have been / really were to have been) home yesterday.   285. He should really be (He really ought to be) here at 5 p. m. tomorrow.   286. Because (As/ Since) it is raining, I must (have to) take an umbrella.   287. The man with the broken arm asked, "When will I be able to write again?"   288. You should have gone (ought to have gone / were to have gone / were supposed to have gone) to the dentist on Monday. Why weren't you there?   289. We weren't allowed to (weren't permitted to / were forbidden to) sit on the table at school.   290. She should make (is to make / is supposed to make) her bed, but she doesn't have to (need not) tidy up her room.   291. If I had lost the book, I would have been forced to (would have had to / would have been compelled to) buy a new one.   292. I am not allowed

to (am not permitted to / am forbidden to / may not) jump on the bed at home.
293. d) 294. b) 295. d) 296. c) 297. b) 298. c) 299. a) 300. c)
301. a) 302. d) 303. a) 304. c) 305. d) 306. c) 307. c) 308. a)
309. d) 310. c) 311. d) 312. c) 313. d) 314. b) 315. b) 316. c)
317. c)

Gerunds

21. Gerunds

1. seeing   2. to see   3. waiting   4. not to touch   5. to lock; going   6. not to speak   7. smoking   8. showing; to work   9. walking; to let   10. playing; doing   11. overhearing   12. smoking   13. to smoke   14. going; saying   15. He has improved his French by learning . . .   16. Alfred succeeded in defeating . . .   17. Father could not help laughing heartily.   18. I insist on your coming at once.   19. I did not mind his opening the window.   20. Tommy, stop talking!   21. Father is fond of reading the . . .   22. After having returned from school, Tom did . . .   23. The girl got an expensive stamp by paying a great . . .   24. Before going to school, we say . . .   25. Nobody can be put into jail before having been tried.   26. He left the room without saying a word.   27. Charles got a prize for having written the . . .   28. After having arrived in London, Tom . . .   29. Swimming is healthy.   30. The Normans continued speaking French.   31. He finished speaking and . . .   32. We are looking forward to reading your . . .   33. They don't allow smoking in . . .   34. He is thinking of leaving his job and going to . . .   35. He was accused of stealing cars.   36. Do stop talking; I am trying to finish a . . .   37. The police accused him of setting fire to the house, but he denied having been there.   38. I couldn't help laughing.   39. Traveling by ship is more pleasant than traveling by . . .   40. I have always liked learning poems.   41. I prefer walking.   42. Billy was very proud of having won a . . .   43. I have finished writing a . . .   44. I don't mind your going alone.   45. Nobody will prevent you from doing that.   46. You can't accuse him of being lazy.   47. After having finished his work, he . . .   48. Tom frightened me by banging the . . .   49. You may depend on my coming in time.   50. Please excuse my being in a great hurry.   51. Seeing is believing.   52. I hate listening to such talk.   53. Monika is proud of being a German.   54. What is the meaning of . . .   55. Writing books is . . .   56. She remembers going to . . .   57. Did you remember to lock . . .   58. After spending two days arguing about where to go for their holidays, they decided not to go anywhere.   59. He said, "I'm terribly sorry for keeping you waiting."   60. The teacher began by telling us . . .   61. Would you like to come to . . .   62. What about buying two . . .   63. What about coming with . . .   64. When would you like to start?   65. Let's wait until it stops raining.   66. He succeeded in climbing out . . .   67. Remember to bring your balls.   68. What about having a . . .   69. After spending/ having spent a week in the cottage, he decided that he didn't really enjoy living in . . .   70. The town was captured without a shot being fired.   71. You still have a lot to learn if you'll forgive my saying so.   72. Why do you keep on looking back?   73. Is he afraid of walking home . . .   74. We regret his having given an impolite answer.   75. Do you remember hearing that . . .   76. The story was so interesting that the girls stopped talking to listen to it.   77. We are interested in going to the cinema.   78. They don't allow girls to wear trousers . . .   79. They don't allow girls wearing trousers . . .   80. Did she remember to phone you . . .   81. Do you understand our having phoned them yesterday?   82. She watched TV before doing her

Gerunds

... 83. Could they imagine your being / having been on television? 84. Please forgive them for having hurt you. 85. Linda, stop eating! 86. Mr. Smith didn't permit talking in ... 87. I sewed my dress without using a ... 88. After having gone to school for one year, I could write ... 89. Do you think you'll succeed in getting up at 5 a. m. ? 90. They'll always prefer drinking milk to drinking rum. 91. He didn't mind my reading his book. 92. Would they mind helping him ... 93. Does he feel like cleaning his room? 94. Helping you wash ... 95. Would you mind telling me ... 96. They didn't allow their children to watch television. 97. Sally, stop running! 98. After having taken English for four years, she could ... 99. Riding a boat ... 100. He was susected of shooting the man. 101. I'll always dislike writing letters. 102. I didn't mind their smoking ... 103. I read her letter before writing an ... 104. Did you remember to buy shoes ... 105. During their walk they stopped to have a ... 106. They don't permit running in ... 107. He regrets her going / having gone home. 108. I am interested in collecting stamps. 109. Do you remember climbing trees ... 110. I understand his having helped her. 111. They will, of course, succeed in getting a good mark. 112. Do you feel like going to bed? 113. Can you imagine my drinking / having drunk oil? 114. He did his homework without asking his ... 115. I regret their having left us so soon. 116. Do you remember reading that ... 117. After having slept for two hours, we ... 118. He is interested in reading many books. 119. Do they feel like going for a picnic? 120. They washed their hands without using soap. 121. Are you proud of being a ... 122. We don't allow cheating on ... 123. We understand her running / having run away from home. 124. Would he mind showing ... 125. ... the children stopped playing in the snow to see it. 126. I'll succeed in writing a book. 127. Could he imagine your sitting / having sat on a camel? 128. I love riding a pony. 129. She had seen him often before talking to him. 130. Please forgive me for being / having been late. 131. He always liked helping his ... 132. We won't permit our boy to smoke at ... 133. Do they always remember to go to ... 134. They didn't mind our talking loudly. 135. Watching birds is an ... 136. He does most of the talking. 137. She likes working in the office. 138. ... had stopped helping him. 139. ... stopped to help us. 140. ... stopped helping his ... 141. I always like seeing a ... 142. Right now I'd prefer to be alone. 143. I dislike taking such ... 144. He avoided meeting her ... 145. ... he kept on talking. 146. Would you like to go for ... 147. I want you to read that ... 148. I remember seeing / having seen the ... 149. My mother always expects me to make my bed. 150. If you don't stop making that ... 151. I couldn't help feeling sorry ... 152. I like playing records. 153. Will you please remember to bring me ... 154. Why can't you help me to make the ... 155. My brother's trying to draw a ... 156. If we stop to buy a ... 157. Don't try to move your ... 158. ... she hadn't remembered to phone him ... 159. I can't help singing that ... 160. ... to remember going / having gone to ... 161. I'm fond of drawing pictures and I'd like you to draw one, too. 162. I hope you enjoyed watching

Gerunds

the film.   163. Did you forget to write the ...   164. ... stopped crying.   165. ... we stopped to help her.   166. She wants to go for ...   167. He prefers eating chocolate ...   168. ... kept on walking.   169. He avoided seeing me ...   170. She would hate to hurt her ...   171. We did not mind going to ...   172. ... he finished writing the ...   173. ... Susan to read the ...   174. Please try to tell me ...   175. I'd like to hear that ...   176. Don't forget to write your ...   177. Stop talking when ...   178. Father hates being late.   179. I couldn't help crying when ...   180. Try talking without ...   181. ... regret taking/having taken Susan's ...   182. Father used to take the ...   183. We advised him to go to ...   184. ... we'll forget to leave on time.   185. We were used to going to ...   186. We used to go to ...   187. ... required us to tell them ...   188. ... try going to ...   189. We stopped to help the ...   190. I was used to working late ...   191. I advised writing a ...   192. My sister likes taking pictures ...   193. ... me to learn the ...

22. Participles

1. . . . pictures taken long ago.   2. The girl, waiting for the bus, was . . .   3. Knowing that we had . . .   4. . . . desk, writing a letter.   5. Snatching his coat, the boy ran out . . .   6. . . . and found ourselves surrounded . . .   7. The woman, waiting at the bus stop, was very . . .   8. . . . outside, lying in the sunshine.   9. . . . pictures drawn by a . . .   10. I found the girls acting very . . .   11. After having finished /After finishing her homework, . . .   12. . . . brother, riding a bicycle.   13. Seeing the spider, . . .   14. Knowing that the . . .   15. If asked her name and address, the little girl couldn't . . .   16. . . . cake baked by . . .   17. . . . us in the coming year.   18. We like children swimming.   19. Not seeing the baby, I . . .   20. . . . because of her screaming child.   21. Though paying / Though having paid for the lesson, . . .   22. We found the stolen car.   23. Seeing that she wouldn't catch the bus, the girl stopped running.   24. Yelling that she was late, the teenager ran . . .   25. The boy, writing a letter, didn't . . .   26. . . . cars given to us . . .   27. Feeling lonely, I went . . .   28. . . . while listening to . . .   29. . . . found her mother sleeping.   30. Hoping to get . . .   31. Saying good-night to the children, the mother left . . .   32. After having eaten / After eating our meal, . . .   33. Looking through . . .   34. While taking a . . . / The man sang while taking a shower.   35. Though wanting to go . . .   36. Seeing the mouse, the . . .   37. . . . cat sitting in a tree.   38. If taken at once, the medicine will . . .   39. Not being told/Not having been told exactly . . .   40. . . . man riding on . . .   41. . . . found the doctor helping him.   42. . . . horse, ridden by . . .   43. After saying / After having said "good-bye", our friends drove away.   44. Taking his money, the man went to the shop.   45. Having closed the door, the man locked it.   46. . . . boy hiding from them.   47. . . . baby held by its mother.   48. . . . away, leaving the . . .   49. Not feeling good, the child . . .   50. The work having been completed, the . . .   51. Having gone to bed . . .   52. After having bathed / After bathing the baby, the mother put it to bed.   53. Catching / Having caught the ball, the player ran to . . .   54. . . . bird caught by . . .   55. Having rained, the . . .   56. . . . found themselves surrounded by . . .   57. Though expecting her child to phone in the evening, the mother waited . . .   58. Taking a pencil, the child drew . . .   59. Thinking it would . . .   60. Having taken her shower, the woman went to bed.   61. After having finished / After finishing their job, the men ate . . .   62. Not wanting to be late, the man . . .   63. If drunk too quickly, the cold milk will . . . .   64. Until coming here, I didn't . . .   65. Climbing on a chair, the baby started . . .   66. . . . dirt, swept under . . .   67. After drinking / After having drunk her milk, the girl was happy.   68. Thinking the baby . . .   69. Opening the door, the woman looked outside.   70. . . . sour unless drunk at once. / Unless drunk at once, the milk . . .   71. When painted, the house looked pretty.   72. Though having started / Though starting her homework early, the girl wasn't . . .   73. After having been baked / Having been baked, the cake was . . .   74. . . . pictures taken long ago.   75. Not knowing where to turn, the driver . . .   76. Not having worked

Participles 53

hard for the test, the children were . . .   77. . . . wind, as if held back . . .   78. The sky being so dark, we . . .   79. After having caught / After catching / Having caught the bird, the cat . . .   80. . . . die unless given the medicine . . .   81. The rain finished, we . . .   82. . . . till having heard that . . .   83. Though eating twice as much as anyone else, the girl didn't . . .   84. If performed faithfully every day, the exercises will help you lose weight.   85. Not wishing to be alone, the . . .   86. . . . homework, written the . . .   87. After having been read / After being read/Having been read, the book was returned . . .   88. Not seeing where we . . .   89. Having thrown the ball, . . .   90. . . . night, each going his . . .   91. Hoping to be invited . . .   92. The music being so loud, . . .   93. . . . leg, swinging it around / Holding his child by its leg, the father swung it around.   94. If forced to eat, the child will vomit.   95. . . . dress, especially sewn for her.   96. The tree having been cut / being cut down,   . . . / After having been cut / After being cut down, the tree was made . . .   97. Not being able to buy anything cheap, the woman went . . .   98. Expecting you to be . . .   99. Though watered every day, the garden dried . . .   100. I cried, hiding my . . .   101. Having understood the sentences, the children were happy.   102. Not being able to go to sleep, I . . .   103. Expecting to be hit, the . . .   104. After having slept / After sleeping / Having slept for a long time, the woman felt better.   105. If practised every day, the English words . . .   106. Not wanting to impose, the visitors didn't . . .   107. Though having studied very hard, the pupil failed . . .   108. We heard her talking to . . .   109. . . . time taking care . . .   110. . . . piano being played by . . .   111. . . . baby sleeping quietly.   112. A dog came running up . . .   113. . . . me standing at . . .   114. After having eaten / After eating her food, Tina left . . .   115. We cleaned up, singing as we worked.   116. Opening the door, the father saw . . .   117. Having seen so many churches, the tourists no longer . . .   118. My mother heard me speaking with the man.   119. I'll have my hair cut next week. / I'm getting my hair cut next week.   120. The man kept his car running.   121. Can the boy make himself understood?   122. I heard my name being called.   123. She wants the room cleaned up (tidied up) by this evening.   124. I feel the ants crawling up my legs.   125. The man had his shoes repaired.   126. I want it taken away immediately.   127. I had my tooth pulled last week.   128. We will have our car washed next week.   129. Having been fed the best meat, the cat didn't want to eat the leftovers from the table.   130. The boy came home, followed by his friends.

23. The infinitive with and without "to"

1. go   2. to help   3. to tell   4. to be   5. to leave   6. tell   7. to get   8. to go
9. to get   10. to wear   11. go   12. to let   13. to be   14. to return   15. jump
16. to see   17. to want   18. to help   19. come   20. to open   21. to leave
22. to walk   23. wear   24. to bake   25. to pass   26. go   27. to load/load
28. to stop   29. to tell   30. to go   31. to read   32. leave   33. to tell   34. to do   35. to take   36. strike 37. to enter   38. to be   39. to come   40. use
41. to rain   42. to read; to write   43. to go on   44. take   45. to remind
46. to understand   47. to open   48. work   49. to go   50. to go   51. to stop
52. to be   53. to go   54. write   55. to see   56. to help   57. to do   58. to know   59. to come   60. go   61. eat   62. to catch   63. to write   64. blow
65. to do   66. to be   67. tell   68. to come   69. put   70. to go   71. come
72. to swim   73. to open   74. to marry   75. to be   76. drink   77. to work
78. to write   79. to hurry   80. to wear   81. to be   82. to be   83. eat   84. to get   85. to stay   86. to come   87. pay   88. to drink   89. to swim   90. to marry   91. do; do   92. to pass   93. I showed him how to write his name.
94. The teachers decided where to have their picnic.   95. We were pleased to hear that you were coming.   96. I bet she'd be surprised to get a letter!   97. How often have we told you not to say that word?   98. Did he understand how to get to Bonn?   99. Did they tell you when to come?   100. We didn't remember whether to come today or tomorrow.   101. We had hoped to have left early. /We had hoped to leave early.   102. Did the children know where to buy pancakes?
103. Has he remembered what to ask them?   104. We forgot which road to take.
105. Has the new mother found out when to bathe the baby?   106. Did the boy forget how to unlock the door?   107. Has the girl understood why it is important to brush her teeth?   108. Did you decide whom to tell the story?   109. We were sorry to hear that you had been ill.   110. I'd be glad to shake his hand.
111. Has the man discovered what to take home?   112. Did they ask where to meet us?   113. Do the children know which man to ask for help if they are lost?
114. I would be delighted to go with you!   115. He was surprised to see his son driving a car.   116. They must have decided whether to eat now or later.   117. I found out whom to ask for money.   118. Did you ask to take John with you?
119. How did you know whether to speak or to stay silent?   120. We would be delighted to visit them.   121. Did your teacher tell you which words to learn?
122. I wonder when to phone her.   123. They showed us whom to help.
124. She didn't know where to turn for help.   125. Has the man thought of what to give his wife for her birthday?   126. The last person to be outside is a donkey.
127. She supposed him to be sleeping.   128. We found it to be very difficult to do.   129. The only person to finish the race was a big boy.   130. Did you estimate it to cost too much?   131. We considered that matter to be finished.
132. It was difficult for me to write a letter in German.   133. Are you ready to take the test? / Are you prepared to take the examination?   134. I expect him to be nice.
135. The people would hate you to be late.   136. Do you promise to help me

The infinitive with and without "to"

tomorrow? 137. He would be happy to have your picture. 138. We would like you to come again soon. / We want you to come again soon. 139. You don't have to go there tomorrow. / You need not go there tomorrow. 140. I would like my son to be a doctor. 141. The man asked me to help him. 142. I would love to go with you. 143. Would you prefer to drink wine? 144. The woman asked to speak to you. 145. He is looking for a possibility to get there. 146. You seem to be growing up so quickly. 147. I implore you to help me. 148. Would you be surprised to meet her here? 149. We are waiting for the rain to stop. 150. He chose to go along.

24. Adverbial clauses

1. When Carl turned the radio off, we . . . / Carl turned the radio off so that we couldn't . . .   2. After Carl had turned the radio off, we couldn't . . .   3. After Tom had eaten ten pieces of cake, his . . .   4. Although/Though Father was very busy, he . . .   5. . . . money so that we can . . .   6. If I had gone to school earlier, I would . . .   7. . . . mother so that she would . . .   8. When/Whenever Dan was not nice, he was bad.   9. . . . corner until/till you come.   10. . . . chair so that it . . .   11. After the baby had climbed onto the chair, it . . . / . . . chair so that it . . .   12. The tree died, although/though/after we had watered it.   13. . . . now so that we can . . .   14. If she had 20,- DM, she would . . .   15. . . . paper so that you can . . .   16. Since/Because Mother bought a dishwasher, we . . .   17. Since Daniel moved to Bonn, he . . .   18. Although/Though the food smelled bad, the women ate it.   19. Since/As/Because it was raining, we . . .   20. Since/As/Because/When/Whenever we were very tired, we . . .   21. If he went to school, he . . .   22. . . . stop, when/ although/though/since/because she couldn't . . .   23. When/Whenever/ Since/Because Susan got a "2", she . . .   24. While Mother was cooking, Father . . .   25. Since/As/Because Harry wanted to write letters, he bought paper.   26. Since/Because Linda liked the colour red, she bought . . .   27. . . . sports that he won . . .   28. Whenever/When we come to town, we . . .   29. . . . pretty that she became . . .   30. Although/Though we helped him, he got . . .   31. . . . tests that he always . . .   32. . . . twice since she moved . . .   33. . . . time that I must . . .   34. . . . person that everyone . . .   35. . . . cinema that we had . . .   36. Because Dan liked cars, he . . .   37. While we were talking on the phone, the . . .   38. Although Tom wanted a new car, he . . .   39. Since White knocked the bar down, Lee . . .   40. Until Dick bought a Ford, he . . .   41. Don was such a stupid person that he . . .   42. If Ben helped his mother, she . . .   43. Whenever we see our friends, we . . .   44. After Linda had got the bad test back, she cried.   45. Tom is so tall that he . . .   46. . . . loudly so that we . . .   47. Since Tom talked to me yesterday, I . . .   48. Before you could take the bus, you . . .   49. When Father had a cold, he . . .   50. . . . written so many letters that her . . .   51. . . . passed since we . . .   52. . . . book so that I . . .   53. If they had finished reading the book, they . . .   54. Though she hadn't started to read the book, she . . .   55. After we had read the book, we . . .   56. When it gets dark, we . . .   57. Because he ate too much, he . . .   58. . . . book because it . . .   59. When the desks are dirty, we . . .   60. When Helen left the room, the . . .   61. . . . happy because he . . .   62. . . . dark because/when it was raining. / When it was dark it was raining.   63. . . . play when Robert . . .   64. He cried because he . . .   65. When he reached . . .   66. He failed, though he . . .   67. If you are good, you . . .   68. If you walk quickly, you . . .   69. Though you walk quickly, you . . .   70. If you want to grow tall, you . . .   71. Though you want to go home, you . . .   72. . . . dirty, though it was . . .   73. If he wants to go to the university, he . . .   74. . . . policeman if I got . . .   75. He got lost, though he had . . .   76. If Mother

Adverbial clauses

went to the grocer's, she . . .   77. She was happy, though she got . . .   78. If we go home now, we . . .   79. When it strikes 8, we . . .   80. . . . ill because you . . .   81. Though he is a teacher, he . . .   82. . . . cried because she had . . .   83. If you are good, you . . .   84. When/Because the film was over, we . . .   85. If they all go, we will. . .   86. . . . suddenly because/ when a person . . .   87. If I met the film star, I . . .   88. If you did your lessons, you . . .   89. Though she tried very hard, she failed.   90. . . . time because she failed . . .   91. If he works hard, he . . .   92. Because they had worked hard, they . . .   93. When some people had got in, the . . .   94. Since/As/Because the girls didn't study, they . .   95. Until/ Although/Though/When/Till I was three years old, I couldn't talk.   96. . . . quickly so that he . . .   97. Since/As/Because the lady was standing, I . . .   98. Although/Though she looked like 16, she . . . / She looked like 16, although/though she was . . .   99. When/Because/ As/Since the boy saw the mouse, he . . .   100. . . . was so very tired that she . . .   101. Because/As/Since/When it was dark, we . . .   102. Although/Though it was dark, we . . .   103. Because/Since/As it was dark, we lit candles so that the children . . .   104. . . . radio so that I could . . . / When/Since/Because I turned off the radio, I could . . .   105. They were so very tired that they went . . . / Since/Because/As/Whenever they were very tired, they . . .   106. Although/ Though it was raining, the children . . .   107. When we went swimming, it . . . / We went swimming because/since/while/whenever it was so hot.   108. . . . records, although/though/until/till he had little money.   /Since/Because he bought records, he had . . .   109. . . . ring while/when I was reading . . .   110. . . . phone because/since/after I had heard . . . / Before I went to the phone, I had . . .   111. . . . grade, although/though he had . . .   112. Since/As/Because I have no dress to wear, I . . .   113. Since/Because/As we bought a dishwasher, we . . . / . . . dishwasher so that we don't . . .   114. While Mother was preparing the food, the . . .   115. It was so cold that the . . .   116. Although/Though it was rainy, we had . . .   117. . . . hard so that they should . . . / Since/As/Because the girls worked hard, they . . .   118. . . . over because/since it is her . . .   119. . . . voice that she had . . .   120. If they installed a new traffic light, a lot . . .   121. Before   122. until   123. while   124. After/ Since/As/Because   125. since

Vocabulary (Vokabeln)

a	ein
ability	Fähigkeit
a bit	ein bißchen
able	fähig
about	über
above	über
absent	abwesend, fehlen
absolutely	absolut, vollkommen, vollständig
absurd	albern, lächerlich
accident	Unfall
accordingly	gemäß
accuse of	beschuldigen
accustomed to	gewohnt zu tun
ache	Schmerz
acknowledge	anerkennen, eingestehen
across	über
act	Auftritt, Aufzug, sich benehmen
action, to take	in die Tat setzen, in Bewegung setzen
active	aktiv, belebt
actor	Schauspieler
additionally	zusätzlich
address	Adresse
adjective	Adjektiv, Eigenschaftswort
adjust to	anpassen
admit	gestehen, zugeben
adore	anbeten, verehren
advantage of	im Vorteil sein
adverb	Adverb, Umstandswort
adverbial clauses	Adverbialsätze
advice, to take	einen Rat befolgen
advise	beraten, raten
afford	leisten
afraid	ängstlich, besorgt
afraid of	Angst haben vor
after	nachdem
afternoon	Nachmittag
afterwards	nachher
again	wieder
age, of	mündig sein, volljährig
ago	vor
agree	sich einigen
agree on	sich einigen, zustimmen
agree to	genehmigen, zustimmen
aim	Absicht, erstreben, zielen

Vocabulary (Vokabeln)

air	Luft
airplane	Flugzeug
alarm clock	Wecker
alcohol	Alkohol
all	alle
all in all	im ganzen
allow	erlauben
allowed	gestatten
all the same	ganz gleich, nichtsdestoweniger
almighty	allmächtig
almost	beinahe, fast
alone	allein
along	mit
already	schon
also	auch
alternative	Alternative, Wahl
although	obwohl
altogether	durchaus, ganz und gar
always	immer
am	bin
amazed at	erstaunt, überrascht
amazing	höchst erstaunlich, verblüffend
ambition	Ehrgeiz
ambitious	ehrgeizig
amount to	hinauslaufen, sich belaufen
amuse	sich gut unterhalten, vergnügen
and	und
angry	böse, sauer
animal	Tier
annoy	belästigen, irritieren, stören
another	noch eine
answer	Antwort, beantworten
ant	Ameise
anticipate	erhoffen, erwarten
anxious	bedacht, besorgt
any	keine, welche
anyhow	immerhin, jedenfalls
anyone	irgend etwas, irgend jemand
anyway	auf irgendeine Weise, wie dem auch sei
apart from	abgesehen von
apologize for	sich entschuldigen, Vergebung bitten
apparently	anscheinend, offenbar
appear	erscheinen
apple	Apfel

Vocabulary (Vokabeln)

appreciate	schätzen, würdigen
approach	sich nähern
approve	gut heißen, zustimmen
apt	geneigt
are	sind
argue	diskutieren
arise	entstehen, sich erheben
around	herum, rum
arrange	anordnen, ordnen
arrest	verhaften
arrive	ankommen
artist	Künstler
as	da, weil
ashamed of	sich schämen
ask	fragen
ask for	bitten um
asleep	schlafen
assert	bestehen auf, geltend machen
assist in	unterstützen
as soon as	sobald als
assume	annehmen
assure	versichern
astonished at	sich wundern, überrascht
astonishing	erstaunlich
at any rate	auf jeden Fall
at least	wenigstens
at once	sofort
attempt	Versuch, versuchen
attention	Aufmerksamkeit
attentive	aufmerksam
attractive	reizend
aunt	Tante
authority	Autorität, Vollmacht
autograph	Unterschrift
autumn	Herbst
avoid	meiden, vermeiden
awake	aufwecken, wecken
away	weg
awful	schrecklich
awkward	peinlich, ungeschickt
back	zurück
bad	schlecht
bag	Sack
bake	backen

Vocabulary (Vokabeln)

balcony	Balkon
to bang	schlagen
bar	Tafel
barely	kaum, knapp
bark	bellen
barrow	Schubkarre
basket	Korb
bath	Bad
bathe	baden
bathroom	Badezimmer
be	sein
beach	Strand
be against	dagegen sein
bear	Bär, geboren, tragen
beat	schlagen, übertreffen
beautiful	schön
because	da, weil
become	werden
bed	Bett
bedroom	Schlafzimmer
beer	Bier
be for	dafür sein
before	vor
beg	bitten um
beget	zeugen
beggar	Bettler
begin	anfangen
begin by	damit anfangen
behave	sich benehmen
behold	ansehen, betrachten
believe in	glauben an
bell	Glocke
belong	gehören
below	unter
bend	beugen, biegen
benefit from	Vorteil ziehen aus
beseech	anflehen
besides	außerdem
best	beste
bet	wetten
better	besser, verbessern
bicycle	Fahrrad
bid	befehlen, bieten
big	groß

Vocabulary (Vokabeln)

bike	Fahrrad, Rad
bill	Rechnung
bind	binden
bird	Vogel
birthday	Geburtstag
biscuits	Plätzchen
bite	beißen
bitter	bitter, schmerzhaft
black	schwarz
blame	tadeln
blame for	einem Schuld geben an
bleat	blöken
bleed	bluten
blind	blind
blouse	Bluse
blow	blasen
blue	blau
bluntly	barsch, grob, stumpf
board	Brett, Tafel
boast	angeben, prahlen
boast about	sich rühmen
boat	Boot
body	Körper
bombs	Bomben
bone	Knochen
book	Buch
boots	Stiefel
boring	langweilig
born	geboren
boss	Chef, Vorgesetzter
bother about	sich aufregen über, sich bemühen
bound	bestimmt unterwegs nach
be bound to	wird unbedingt
box	Schachtel
boy	Junge
boyfriend	Freund
brains	Intelligenz, Verstand
brave	mutig
bread	Brot
break	brechen, zerbrechen
breakfast	Frühstück
breed	züchten
bribe	bestechen
briefly	kürzlich, kurz zusammengefaßt

bright	glänzend, hell, schlau
bring	bringen
broadcast	senden
broken	zerbrochen
brother	Bruder
brown	braun
brush	bürsten, putzen
bubble	Blase
build	bauen
building	Gebäude
burden	Last
burglar	Einbrecher
burn	brennen
burst	explodieren, platzen
bus stop	Bushaltestelle
busy	beschäftigt
but	aber
butterfly	Schmetterling
buy	kaufen
by	bis, von
by far	bei weitem
cage	Käfig
cake	Kuchen
calculate	berechnen, kalkulieren
call	rufen
camel	Kamel
can	können
cancer	Krebs
candle	Kerze
candy	Süßigkeiten
cannot but	kann nicht anders als, kann nicht umhin zu
can't help	kann nicht anders als
can't stand	kann nicht aushalten, kann nicht ausstehen
capable of	fähig, imstande sein zu
capacity	Aufnahmefähigkeit, Umfang
captain	Kapitän, Mannschaftsführer
capture	gefangennehmen, fangen
car	Auto
cards	Karten
care	sorgen, Sorgfalt
care about	besorgt sein, sich etwas daraus machen
care for	sich kümmern um, sorgen für

Vocabulary (Vokabeln)

careful	achtsam, sorgfältig
careless	unvorsichtig
care to	Lust haben zu, mögen
carpet	Teppich
carry	tragen
cast	werfen
castle	Schloß
cat	Katze
catch	fangen, kriegen
caterpillar	Raupe
cathedral	Dom
cause	Anlaß, Grund, verursachen
cease	aufhören
certain	bestimmt, sicher
certain of	einer Sache gewiß sein
certainly	gewiß, sicherlich, unzweifelhaft, zweifellos
chair	Stuhl
to chance	wagen, sich zufällig ereignen
chance of	Aussicht auf, Gelegenheit
chancellor	Kanzler
change	ändern
charm	Liebreiz
charming	entzückend, reizend
chase	jagen
cheap	billig
cheat	betrügen, mogeln, pfuschen
cheek	Wange
cheese	Käse
chew	kauen
chewing gum	Kaugummi
chickens	Hühner
chiefly	hauptsächlich
child	Kind
children	Kinder
Chinese	chinesisch
chocolate	Schokolade
choice	Auswahl, Wahl
choose	aussuchen, wählen
Christmas	Weihnachten
church	Kirche
cigar	Zigarre
cigarette	Zigarette
cinema	Kino

Vocabulary (Vokabeln)

circular	rund
city	Stadt
claim	beanspruchen, behaupten
clap	klatschen
class	Klasse
classroom	Klassenzimmer
clean	gänzlich, rein, säubern, sauber
clear	klar
clearly	gänzlich, ganz und gar, völlig
clever	gescheit, klug, schlau
clever at	geschickt in
climb	klettern, steigen
cling	festhalten, sich klammern
clock	Uhr
close	eng, nah, schließen
closely	genau, scharf
clothes	Bekleidung
cloudy	bewölkt
coat	Mantel
coffee	Kaffee
coin	Münze
cold	Erkältung, kalt
collect	sammeln
collector	Sammler
college	Uni
colour	Farbe
colourful	bunt
comb	kämmen
come	kommen
comfortable	bequem
command	Befehl, befehlen
comment	Bemerkung machen, Kommentar
common	alltäglich, gewöhnlich
compel	zwingen
complain	aboutbeklagen über
complete	erledigen, ganz, vervollständigen
completely	ganz, völlig
complicated	kompliziert
compulsion	Zwang
concentrate on	sich konzentrieren auf
concert	Konzert
concession	Einräumung, Zugeständnis
condition	Zustand
conditional	Bedingung, Konditional

Vocabulary (Vokabeln)

cone	Speiseeis
congradulate	beglückwünschen
conjunction	Bindewort, Konjunktion
conscious of	einer Sache bewußt sein
consent	zustimmen
consequently	folgerichtig
consider	der Meinung sein, erwägen, überlegen
considerably	bedeutend, beträchtlich
consist of	bestehen aus
continually	ununterbrochen
continue	fortsetzen
control	Gewalt, Kontrolle
convenient	günstig, passend
convince of	überzeugen von
cook	Koch, kochen
cookies	Plätzchen
cool	kühl
cope with	etwas bewältigen, mit etwas fertig werden
corn	Mais
corner	Ecke
correct	korrigieren, richtige
cost	kosten
cottage	Hütte
count	zählen, Zahlen
count on	sich verlassen auf
counter	Theke
country	Land
courage	Mut
courageous	mutig
cousin	Kusine
cover	bedecken
cowardly	ängstlich, feige
crab	Krabbe
crashed	eingestürzt, zerbrochen
craving	Verlangen
crazy	verrückt
crazy about	verrückt nach
cream	Krem, Sahne
creep	kriechen, schleichen
cross	überqueren
crowning	Krönung
cry	weinen
cup	Tasse
cupboard	Schrank

Vocabulary (Vokabeln)

curious	neugierig
curtain	Vorhang
cut	Abkürzung, schneiden
cut out	aufhören, ausschneiden, unterlassen, weglassen
daily	täglich
dance	Tanz, tanzen
in danger of	Gefahr laufen
dangerous	gefährlich
dare	wagen
dark	dunkel
dash	schnell laufen, wegeilen
date	Datum, Termin
daughter	Tochter
day	Tag
dead	tot
deal	austeilen, handeln
a great deal	Menge, sehr viel, Viel
dear	lieb, teuer
decency	Anstand
decent	anständig
decide on	sich entscheiden für
decision	Beschluß, Entscheidung
declare	angeben, aussagen, behaupten
deep	tief
deeply	sehr
deer	Reh
defeat	besiegen, schlagen
defend	sich verteidigen
defer	sich beugen, nachgeben, verschieben
definitely	bestimmt, deutlich
delay	verzögern
delicious	lecker
delighted	entzückt
delight in	Freude haben an, Spaß haben an
be delighted in	sich freuen über
demand	verlangen
dentist	Zahnarzt
deny	dementieren, leugnen, verneinen
depend on	abhängen von, sich darauf verlassen
desire	verlangen, wünschen
desk	Schreibtisch
determination	Entschlossenheit
determine	bestimmen, entscheiden, unbedingt tun wollen
detest	verabscheuen

Vocabulary (Vokabeln)

devote to	aufopfern für, sich hingeben an, widmen
dial	wählen
die	sterben
difference between	Unterschied zwischen
different	anders, verschieden
difficult	schwierig
difficulty in	Schwierigkeit haben; es schwierig finden, etwas zu tun
dig	graben
dining-room	Eßzimmer
dinner	Hauptmahlzeit
direct	direkt, gerade
direction	Richtung
dirt	Dreck, Schmutz
dirty	dreckig
disappeared	verschwunden
disappointed about	enttäuscht über
disapprove of	mißbilligen
discontinue	aufhören, unterbrechen
discover	entdecken
disease	Krankheit
disgust	anekeln
disgusted	sich über einen ärgern
dish	Teller
dishes	Geschirr
dishwasher	Geschirrspülmaschine
dislike	nicht mögen
distance	Entfernung
distinct	klar
distinguish	sich auszeichnen, unterscheiden
in distress	in Not
disturbed	gestört
dive	tauchen
do	machen, tun
doctor	Arzt
dog	Hund
doll	Puppe
donkey	Esel
door	Tür
doubt about	zweifeln an
down	'runter
drastic	drastisch
draw	malen, ziehen
drawers	Schubladen

Vocabulary (Vokabeln)

dread	fürchten
dreadful	schrecklich
dream	Traum, träumen
dream of	träumen von
dress	Kleid
dress 'self	sich anziehen
drink	Getränk, trinken
drive	fahren
driver	Fahrer
drop	fallenlassen
dry	trocken
ducks	Enten
due, duly	angemessen, geziemend
dull, dully	dumm, geistlos, langweilig
during	während
duty	Pflicht
dwell	wohnen
each	jeder
each other	einander
eager	begierig
ear	Ohr
early	früh
earn	verdienen
earth	Erde
Easter	Ostern
easy	einfach, leicht
eat	essen, fressen
edition	Ausgabe
efficient	leistungsfähig, wirksam
effort, to make an	sich anstrengen
egg	Ei
eight	acht
either	entweder
electrician	Elektriker
elephant	Elefant
eleven	elf
else	noch
empty	leer
empty-handed	mit leeren Händen
enable	befähigen
encourage	ermutigen
encouragement	Ansporn, Ermutigung
endeavour	sich bemühen
English	englisch

Vocabulary (Vokabeln)

enjoy	genießen
enough	genug
enter	betreten
enthusiastic about	begeistert über
entirely	durchaus, völlig
entitle	Anspruch haben auf, berechtigt sein zu
envelope	Umschlag
equally	gleich
escape	entfliehen, entkommen
especially	besonders
estimate	schätzen, veranschlagen
eternal	ewig
even	flach, gerade, glatt, noch
(not even)	noch nicht einmal
evening	Abend
ever	je
everlasting	ewig
every	alle, jeder
everybody	jedermann
everyone	jede
everything	alles
everywhere	überall
evidently	einleuchtend, klar, offenbar
exactly	genau
exam	Prüfung
excellent	vorzüglich
excited about	aufgeregt über
exciting	aufregend
exclusively	ausschließlich
excuse	entschuldigen
exercise	üben, Übung
expect	erwarten
expensive	teuer
experience	erfahren, Erfahrung
experience in	Erfahrung in
experiment	Experiment
explain	erklären
extend an invitation	eine Einladung aussprechen
extra	außergewöhnlich, besonder
extremely	äußerst
eye	Auge
fabulous	toll
face	Gesicht
fail	mißlingen, scheitern

Vocabulary (Vokabeln)

fail in	durchfallen
fair	anständig, ehrlich, schön
fairly	recht, ziemlich
faithfully	genau, treu
fall	fallen
fall asleep	einschlafen
fall back on	sich stützen auf, zurückgreifen auf
false	falsch
famous	berühmt
fancy	gern haben, vorstellen
fantastic	toll
far	weit
farm	Bauernhof
farmer	Bauer
fascinating	bezaubernd
fast	schnell
fat	dick
father	Vater
favour	begünstigen, vorziehen
for fear of	aus Furcht vor, da. . . zu befürchten ist
fed up with	satt haben
feed	ernähren, füttern
feel	fühlen, merken, spüren, wahrnehmen
feeling	Gefühl
fence	Gitter, Zaun
festivities	Festlichkeiten
fetch	holen
few	wenig
field	Feld
fight	kämpfen
finally	endlich, zum Schluß
find	feststellen, finden
fine	gut, schön
finish	beenden, fertig machen
finished	fertig, vollendet
fire	abgeben, Feuer
first	erst, zuerst
fish	Fisch
five	fünf
flat	flach
flee	fliehen
fling	schleudern
floor	Fußboden
flower	Blume

Vocabulary (Vokabeln)

fly	fliegen
fog	Nebel
fold	falten
follow	folgen
fond of	gerne mögen
food	Essen
foot	Fuß
for	für, seit
forbid	verbieten
force	zwingen
for certain	sicherlich
forecast	voraussagen
forest	Wald
for example	zum Beispiel
forget	vergessen
forgive	vergeben
fork	Gabel
forsake	verlassen
for sure	gewiß, sicherlich
fortunately	glücklicherweise
four	vier
France	Frankreich
frankly	offen gesagt
free	befreien, frei
freedom	Freiheit
freeze	gefrieren
frequency	Häufigkeit
frequently	häufig
fresh	frisch
Friday	Freitag
friend	Freund
friendly	freundlich
friendship	Freundschaft
frightened of	Angst haben vor
in front of	vor
fruit	Obst
full, fully	voll
fun	es macht Spaß
funny	komisch, lustig
furious	wütend
furniture	Möbel
furthermore	außerdem
future	Zukunft
future perfect	vollendete Zukunft

Vocabulary (Vokabeln)

gain	zunehmen
game	Spiel
gangster	bewaffneter Verbrecher
garden	Garten
geese	Gänse
generally	normalerweise
generous	großzügig
gentle	sanft
German	deutsch
gerund	Gerundium, substantiviertes Verb, Verb als Substantiv gebraucht
get	bekommen, gewinnen, kriegen, veranlassen
get around to	dazukommen, etwas zu tun
get married	heiraten
get off	aussteigen
get up	aufstehen
ghost	Geist
gift	Geschenk
girl	Mädchen
girlfriend	Freundin
give	geben, schenken
give up	aufgeben
glad	froh, glücklich
glad about	erfreut über
glass	Glas
go, goes	fahren, gehen, reisen
goal	Tor, Ziel
go along	mitfahren
God	Gott
gone	weg
good	gut
good at	geschickt in
good-bye	Auf Wiedersehen
go on	fortfahren, weitermachen
grade	Note
grammar	Grammatik
grandfather	Großvater
grandmother	Großmutter
grass	Rasen
grateful for	dankbar für
great	großartig, wichtig
greedy	begierig
green	grün

Vocabulary (Vokabeln)

greet	begrüßen
grind	mahlen, schleifen
grocer	Lebensmittelhändler
ground	Boden, Erde
grow	wachsen
grown-up	Erwachsene
grumble at	murren, nörgeln über
grumpy	mißlaunisch, mürrisch
guarantee	bürgen für, garantieren
guess	abschätzen, erraten
guest	Gast
guilty of	schuldig
gum	Gummi
gun	Gewehr, Schußwaffe
habit of	gewöhnt sein zu, pflegen zu
had better	Sie täten besser zu
hair	Haare
half	halb
half an hour	eine halbe Stunde
half past	halb
hall	Flur
handbag	Handtasche
handkerchief	Taschentuch
handle	bewältigen
handsome	gut aussehend
handwriting	Handschrift
handy	handlich
hang	sich aufhängen, hängen
happen	geschehen
happy	froh
happy about	glücklich über
hard	schwer
hardly	kaum
has	hat
hasty	hastig
hat	Hut
hate	haßen
have	besitzen, haben, veranlassen
he	er
head	Kopf
headmaster	Direktor
healthy	gesund
hear	hören
hear about/of	erfahren von/über, hören

heart, to have the	übers Herz bringen
heartily	aufrichtig, herzlich, innig
heat	Hitze
heavenly	himmlisch
heavy	schwer
help	helfen
helpful	hilfsbereit
helpless	hilflos
hence	daher, deshalb
her	ihr, sie
here	hier
hesitate	zögern
hide	verstecken
high	hoch, laut
highly	sehr, sehr empfehlend, höchst lobend
him	ihm, ihn
hire	anstellen, in Dienst nehmen
his	sein
hit	schlagen
hobby	Hobby, Liebhaberei
hold	halten
hole	Loch
holiday	Ferien, Urlaub
home	nach hause, zu hause
homework	Hausaufgaben
honest	ehrlich
hope	hoffen
hope of	Hoffnung auf
horrified	entsetzt
horse	Pferd
hospital	Krankenhaus
hot	heiß
hour	Stunde
hourly	stündlich
house	Haus
household	Haushalt
how	wie
how about	wie wäre es mit
however	jedoch, wie auch immer
howl	heulen
how long	wie lange
how many	wieviele
how often	wie oft
hungry	hungrig

Vocabulary (Vokabeln)

hunt	jagen, verfolgen
hunter	Jäger
hurry	sich beeilen, hasten
hurry up	sich beeilen
hurt	verletzen, verletzt, wehtun
husband	Ehemann
I	ich
ice-cream	Eis
idea	Idee
idle	faul
if	ob
ill	krank, schlecht
imagine	annehmen, sich vorstellen
immediate	sofort
immensely	unermeßlich
implore	anflehen
impolite	unhöflich
important	wichtig
impose	auferlegen, aufdrängen
impossible	unmöglich
impressive	eindrucksvoll, imponierend
improve	verbessern
in addition	außerdem, noch dazu
in brief	in kurzem, mit wenigen Worten
inch	2,5 cm
inclination	Hang, Neigung
inclined	geneigt
include	einbeziehen, einschließen
in comparison	verglichen mit
in conclusion	schließlich
in contrast	im Gegensatz
incorrectly	falsch, irrtümlich, unrichtig
indeed	tatsächlich
induce	verursachen
inducement	Anreiz, Ansporn
indulge in	gönnen, sich etwas erlauben
in fact	in der Tat, tatsächlich
infinite	unendlich
inform	benachrichtigen
in front of	vor
injure	verletzen
in love	verliebt
in order to	um zu
in other words	mit anderen Worten

Vocabulary (Vokabeln)

in part	teilweise, zum Teil
inquire	sich erkundigen
in short	kurzgefaßt
inside	drin
insist on	bestehen auf
inspector	Aufseher, Inspektor
in spite of	ungeachtet, trotz
install	einrichten, einsetzen, installieren
instead of	anstatt, statt
instinct	Instinkt, Naturanlage
instruct	unterrichten
instructions	Anweisungen, Befehle
in sum	insgesamt, zusammenfaßend
intelligence	Intelligenz, Verstand
intelligent	intelligent, klug
intend	beabsichtigen, vorhaben
intense	heftig, intensiv
intensive pronoun	betonendes Fürwort
intention	Absicht, Vorhaben
interest	Interesse
be interested in	interessiert sein an
take an interest in	sich interessieren für
interesting	interessant
introduce	bekannt machen, vorstellen
invitation	Einladung
invite	einladen
involve	hineinziehen, umfassen
iron	bügeln
is	ist
island	Insel
it	es
Italian	italienisch
its	sein
jail	Gefängnis
job	Arbeitsstelle
joke	Witz
juggler	Jongleur
juicy	saftig
jump	springen
just	eben, gerade, gerecht, mit Recht
justify	rechtfertigen
keen on	erpicht auf, interessiert an, verrückt nach
keep	behalten

Vocabulary (Vokabeln)

keeper	Wärter
keep from	abhalten von, bewahren vor, hindern an
keeping house	Haushalt führen
keep off	abhalten, sich fernbleiben
keep on	anbehalten, beibehalten, fortfahren mit, weitermachen
key	Schlüssel
kick	stoßen, treten
kill	töten
kind	freundlich, gütig, liebenswürdig
kindness	Freundlichkeit, Güte
kind of	sozusagen, was für ein
king	König
kiss	küssen
kitchen	Küche
kite	Drachen
kitten	Kätzchen
kneel	knien
knife	Messer
knock down	niederschlagen, niederwerfen, umstoßen
know	kennen, wissen
know about	etwas verstehen von, im Bilde sein über, wissen über
ladder	Leiter
lady	Dame
lake	See
lamp	Lampe
language	Sprache
lap	schlürfen
large	groß
last	letzte, zuletzt
late	spät
lately	kürzlich, neulich, vor kurzem
laugh	lachen
lay	legen, stellen
lazy	faul
lead	führen
leaf	Blatt
lean	lehnen, stützen
leap	springen
learn	erfahren, lernen
leave	abfahren, abreisen, lassen, verlassen, Urlaub
leave, to beg	um Erlaubnis bitten
leaves	Blätter
lecture	Vortrag
left	links, übriggelassen

Vocabulary (Vokabeln)

leg	Bein
lemon	Zitrone
lend	borgen, leihen
lesson	Unterrichtsstunde
let	erlauben, lassen, vermieten, zulassen
letter	Brief
liable	haftbar, neigen zu
liberty	Erlaubnis, Freiheit, Recht
library	Bibliothek, Bücherei
lick	schlecken
lie	liegen
life, lives	Leben
lift	Aufzug, heben
light	anzünden, leuchten, leicht, Licht
like	mögen
likewise	ebenso, gleichfalls
line	Wäscheleine, Zeile
lion	Löwe
listen	horchen, hör mal zu
listen to	anhören, zuhören
litter	Wurf
little	klein, wenig
live	leben, wohnen
liver	Leber
living-room	Wohnzimmer
load	beladen
loathe	verabscheuen
lock	abschließen
lonely	einsam
long	lang
long for	sich sehnen nach
look	ansehen, aussehen, gucken
look after	aufpassen auf
look at	ansehen
look for	suchen
look forward to	sich freuen auf etwas, mit Erwartung entgegensehen
look like	aussehen, den Anschein haben
lorry	LKW
lose, lost	verlieren, verloren
a lot of	viel
loud	laut
love	lieben
lovely	hübsch, reizend, wunderschön
low	leise, niedrig

Vocabulary (Vokabeln)

lowly	bescheiden
lucky	glücklich
lunch	Mittagessen
lying	liegen
machine	Maschine
mad	verrückt, zornig
main clause	Hauptsatz
mainly	hauptsächlich
maintain	behaupten
make	machen, veranlassen, verursachen, ziehen
make 'self understood	sich verständlich machen
make 'self useful	sich nützlich machen
man, men	Mann, Männer
manage	fertigbringen, verwalten, zuwegebringen, schaffen
manager	Betriebsleiter, Direktor, Verwalter
manner	Art und Weise
many	viel
map	Landkarte, Stadtplan
mark	Note
married	verheiratet
marry	heiraten
master	Herr
matchless	unübertrefflich, unvergleichlich
matter	Angelegenheit
may	kann
maybe	vielleicht
me	mich, mir
meal	Essen, Mahlzeit
mean	beabsichtigen, meinen, vorhaben
means	Geldmittel, Hilfsmittel, Mittel
meat	Fleisch
medal	Medaille
medicine	Medizin
meditate	meditieren
meet	kennenlernen, treffen
men	Männer
mention	erwähnen
merely	bloß, nichts als
merry	fröhlich
mess	Durcheinander, Unordnung
method of	Methode, System, Verfahren
mice	Mäuse
midnight	Mitternacht

Vocabulary (Vokabeln)

might	könnte
mile	Meile (1,6 km.)
milk	Milch
mind	etwas dagegen haben, sich kümmern um, geneigt sein, sich entschließen
minute	Minute
mirror	Spiegel
miss	vermissen, verpassen
missing	fehlend
mistake	Fehler
moment	Augenblick
Monday	Montag
money	Geld
monkey	Affe
month	Monat
monthly	monatlich
morally	moralisch
more	mehr
moreover	außerdem, ferner, übrigens
morning	Morgen
most	meist
mother	Mutter
mountain	Berg
mouse	Maus
mouth	Mund
move	bewegen, umziehen
mow	mähen
much	viel
music	Musik
musical	musikalisch
must	müssen
my	mein
name	Name
namely	nämlich
nap	Nickerchen
narrow	eng
natives	Eingeborene
naturally	natürlich
naughty	böse
near	nah
nearly	beinahe, fast
neat	ordentlich
necessary	notwendig
necessity	Notwendigkeit

Vocabulary (Vokabeln)

necessity for	dringendes Bedürfnis nach
neck	Hals
need	Bedarf, Bedrängnis, brauchen, Grund, Notwendigkeit
need for	Grund haben zu
need not	brauchen nicht
neglect	unterlassen, vernachlässigen
neighbour	Nachbar
neither	keiner, weder — noch
nervous	nervös
nervous about	ängstlich wegen
never	nie
nevertheless	dennoch, nichtsdestoweniger
new	neu
newspaper	Zeitung
next	nächste
nice	nett
niece	Nichte
night	Nacht
nine	neun
nobody	keine
It is no good	Es ist zwecklos; Es nützt nichts.
noise	Geräusch
noisy	laut
noon	Mittag
nor	auch nichts, noch
north	nach Norden
nose	Nase
note	Note
nothing	nichts
notice	bemerken
It is no use	Es ist zwecklos; Es hilft nichts
not much use	wenig Sinn
noun	Hauptwort, Substantiv
now	jetzt
nowadays	heutzutage
nowhere	nirgend wo
number	Zahl
object to	Einspruch erheben, protestieren gegen
objection to	Einspruch/Protest erheben
obligation	Verbindlichkeit, Verpflichtung
oblige	verpflichten, zwingen
obliged	verbunden, verpflichtet
observe	bemerken, beobachten

Vocabulary (Vokabeln)

obtain	bekommen, erreichen, erzielen
obviously	deutlich, klar, offenbar, unverkennbar
occasionally	gelegentlich
occasion for/to	Anlaß zu, Gelegenheit für/zu, Grund
ocean	Ozean
o'clock	Uhr
odd	komisch
of course	natürlich, selbstverständlich
offer	anbieten, zur Verfügung stellen
office	Büro, Praxis
officer	Beamter, Polizist
official	Beamter
often	oft
oil	Öl
old	alt
once	einmal
one	ein
only	einzig, erst, nur
on the contrary	im Gegenteil
on the one hand	einerseits
on the other hand	anderseits
on time	pünktlich
open	auf, offen, öffnen
operation	Operation
opportunity of/to	Gelegenheit zu, günstiger Zeitpunkt
oppose	bekämpfen, dagegen sein, entgegentreten
orange	Apfelsine
order	befehlen, ordnen, regulieren
in order to	um zu
organ	Orgel
or rather	oder vielmals
other	andere
otherwise	andernfalls
ought to	soll
our	unser
out	draußen
outside	draußen, nach draußen
over	über
overcome	besiegen, überwinden
overhear	belauschen, zufällig hören
overjoyed	entzückt, hocherfreut
overtake	einholen, überholen
own	besitzen, eigen
owner	Besitzer, Eigentümer

Vocabulary (Vokabeln)

pack	packen
package	Packung
page	Seite
paint	anmalen, Farbe
painter	Maler
pair	Paar
pancakes	Pfannkuchen
pants	Hosen
paper	Papier, Zeitung
pardon	entschuldigen, verzeihen
parents	Eltern
participle	Partizip, Mittelwort, Verb als Adjektiv gebraucht
particularly	besonders, insbesondere
partly	teils, zum Teil
pass	bestehen, vergehen
passive	intransitives Zeitwort, Leideform, Passiv
past	vergangen, Vergangenheit, Imperfekt
past perfect	Plusquamperfekt, vollendete Vergangenheit
patient	geduldig, Patient
pay	bezahlen, zahlen
pay for	Geld geben für, die Kosten tragen, zahlen
peanut	Erdnuß
pear	Birne
peas	Erbsen
pen	Füller
pencil	Bleistift
pen-friend	Brieffreund
people	Leute
perfect	perfekt, vollkommen
performed	durchgeführt, vollbracht
perhaps	möglicherweise, vielleicht
permission	Erlaubnis
permit	erlauben
permitted	darf, durfte
perpetual	ewig, ständig, unaufhörlich, ununterbrochen
perseverance	Ausdauer
persist in	bestehen auf, fortfahren zu tun
person	Person
personally	persönlich
persuade	überreden, überzeugen
phone	anrufen, Telefon, telefonieren
photo	Foto, Lichtbild
physics	Physik
piano	Klavier

Vocabulary (Vokabeln)

pick	pflücken
picture	Bild
pie	Fruchttorte
piece	Stück
pig	Schwein
pin	Nadel
pipe	Pfeife
pistol	Pistole
place	Ort
plan	beabsichtigen, Pläne schmieden, vorhaben
plane	Flugzeug
plant	Pflanze
plate	Teller
platform	Bahnsteig, Bühne, Plattform
play	spielen
player	Spieler
playground	Schulhof, Spielplatz
pleasant	angenehm
please	bitte, gefallen
pleased with	erfreut über, zufrieden mit
have the pleasure of	das Vergnügen haben zu
take pleasure in	Vergnügen finden an
pocket	Tasche
poem	Gedicht
point	zeigen
There's no point in	Es hat keinen Sinn zu
be on the point of	im Begriff sein zu
point out	aufmerksam machen
pointless	sinnlos
police	Polizei
policeman	Polizeibeamter, Schutzmann
polish	putzen
polite	höflich
politically	politisch
pool	Schwimmbecken
poor	arm, schlecht
popular	populär
position	in der Lage sein
possibility	Möglichkeit
possibility of	Möglichkeit für/zu
possible	denkbar, möglich
possibly	möglicherweise, vielleicht
post-office	Postamt
postpone	aufschieben, verschieben

Vocabulary (Vokabeln)

potatoes	Kartoffeln
pound	Pfund
pour	gießen, schütten
practical	praktisch
practise	üben
precise	genau
prefer	bevorzugen, vorziehen
prepare	vorbereiten
present	Gegenwart, Geschenk, Präsens
present perfect	Perfekt, vollendete Gegenwart
press	aufdrängen, bedrängen, drücken, pressieren
presumably	vermutlich, voraussichtlich, wahrscheinlich
pretend	sich ausgeben für; vortäuschen; tun, als ob
pretty	hübsch, recht, ziemlich
prevent	verhindern, vorbeugen
prevent from	hindern an
previous	vorhergehend
price	Preis
prince	Prinz
print	drucken
prison	Gefängnis
privacy	das Alleinsein, die nötige Ruhe, Zurückgezogenheit
privilege of/to	Sonderrecht, Vergnügen, Es steht mir frei
prize	Gewinn, Preis
probably	vermutlich, wahrscheinlich
problem of	Problem, Schwierigkeit
proceed	fortfahren, vorwärtsgehen
profit by/from	Nutzen ziehen aus
professor	Professor
progressive	Dauerform, Verlaufsform
prohibition	Verbot
project	Plan, Projekt, Vorhaben
promise	Versprechen
pronoun	Fürwort, Pronomen
proper	angebracht, geeignet, passend, richtig
propose	beabsichtigen, vorschlagen
proud	stolz
proud of	stolz auf
prove 'self	beweisen, sich erweisen, sich zeigen
psychologically	psychologisch
pull	ziehen
pull 'self together	sich aufraffen, sich zusammennehmen, sich zusammenreißen
pumps	Pumpe

Vocabulary (Vokabeln)

punctual	pünktlich
punish for	(be)strafen wegen
punishment	Bestrafung, Strafe
pupil	Schüler
purpose	Zweck
push	schieben
put	hinlegen, hintun, stellen
put off	aufschieben, auf die lange Bank schieben, verschieben
put on	anziehen
quarrel about	sich zanken über/um
queen	Königen
queer	komisch, seltsam
question	Frage
quick	rasch, schnell
quiet	leise
quite	gänzlich, völlig
rabbit	Hase, Kaninchen
race	Wettlauf, Wettrennen
rain	Regen, regnen
raincoats	Regenmäntel
rainy	regnerisch
rapidly	rasch, schnell
rarely	selten
rather	etwas, ziemlich
rather than	lieber als
reach	erreichen
read	lesen
ready	bereit, fertig
really	tatsächlich, wirklich
reason	Grund, Ursache
reason for	Grund für
rebuild	wieder aufbauen, wieder herstellen
recall	ins Gedächtnis zurückrufen, sich erinnern
receive	bekommen, erhalten
recently	neulich, vor kurzem
recomment	empfehlen
reckon	rechnen auf/mit, schätzen
recognize	wiedererkennen
recollect	sich erinnern
recommend	empfehlen, raten
record	Rekord, Schallplatte
recover	sich erholen
red	rot

Vocabulary (Vokabeln)

reflexive pronoun	Reflexivpronomen, rückbezügliches Fürwort
refrain from	Abstand nehmen von, sich enthalten, unterlassen
refreshing	erfrischend, erquickend
refrigerator	Kühlschrank
refuse	ablehnen, abschlagen, verweigern
regret	bedauern, bereuen
reject	ablehnen, verwerfen
relative	Verwandter
reliable	zuverlässig
relieved to	erleichtert, leichter zumute werden als
reluctant	abgeneigt, widerwillig
rely on	sich verlassen auf
remain	noch vorhanden sein, übrigbleiben, zurückbleiben
remark	äußern; bemerken; gewahr werden, daß
remember	denken an, sich erinnern, sich ins Gedächtnis zurückrufen
remind	erinnern
rend	zerreißen
repair	reparieren
repeat	wiederholen
reply	antworten, erwidern
report	erzählen, berichten
reportedly	angeblich, es wird berichtet, daß, wie verlautet
request	bitten, ersuchen
require	fordern, verlangen
resent	übelnehmen, verübeln
resist	Widerstand leisten, widerstehen
resolve	Beschluß fassen zu, erklären, lösen
respond	eingehen auf, erwidern, reagieren auf
responsibility	Verantwortung
rest	ruhen, sich erholen, sich lehnen gegen, sich stützen auf
result	Ergebnis, Resultat, sich ergeben, herrühren, zur Folge haben
resume	fortfahren, wieder beginnen
return	erwidern, wiederkehren, zurückkehren, zurückschicken
reward	Belohnung
rid	befreien, freimachen von
ride	fahren, reiten
ridiculous	lächerlich, unsinnig
right	angemessen, passend, Recht, rechte, richtig, Recht haben, gerade, sofort
right away	sofort'

be right in	richtig
right now	gerade jetzt
ring	klingeln, läuten
ring up	anrufen
rise	aufstehen, sich erheben
risk	aufs Spiel setzen, riskieren, wagen
There's no risk of	Es besteht keine Gefahr, daß
river	Fluß
road	Straße
roar	brüllen, laut schreien
rob	stehlen
robbers	Räuber
roll	rollen
rolls	Brötchen, Rollen
roll up	aufrollen
room	Zimmer
round	rund
rub	reiben
rubber	Gummi
rude	ungebildet, unhöflich
rug	kleiner Teppich
rules	Regeln
run	laufen, rennen
run away	weglaufen
runway	Landebahn, Startbahn
rush	rasen, sich beeilen
Russian	russisch
sad	traurig
sad about/at	betrübt über, traurig über
safe	sicher
salad	Salat
sales	Verkäufe
same	derselbe
sandwich	belegtes Butterbrot
satisfied with	zufrieden sein mit
Saturday	Samstag
save	aufheben, bewahren, retten
say, says	erzählen, sagen
scarcely	kaum, schwerlich
scientific	wissenschaftlich
school	Schule
scissors	Schere
scold	schelten
scramble	Drängelei, Rangelei

Vocabulary (Vokabeln)

scream	schreien
sea	Meer, See
seagull	Möwe
seaside	an der See, Meeresküste
season	Jahreszeit
seat	Platz nehmen, Sitzplatz
seat 'self	sich hinsetzen
second	zweite
secret	geheim, Geheimnis
secretary	Sekretärin
see	einsehen, erkennen, sehen, verstehen
see about	besorgen, mal abwarten
see 'self	sich vorstellen, selbst darum kümmern
seek	erbitten, suchen
seem	erscheinen
seldom	selten
selfish	egoistisch, selbstsüchtig
self-pity	Selbstmitleid
sell	verkaufen
send	schicken, senden
sensibly	vernünftig
sentence	Satz
separate 'self	sich lossagen, sich lösen, trennen, sich absondern
September	September
series	Reihe, Serien
serious about	es ernst meinen mit, ernsthaft
services	Gottesdienst
set	legen, setzen
setting	untergehende
settle 'self	ansiedeln, beruhigen, niederlassen
seven	sieben
severe	streng
sew	nähen
shake	schütteln
sharp	punkt, scharf
shave	rasieren
she	sie
shed	vergießen, verlieren
sheep	Schaf
sheet	Bettlaken
shelf	Brett, Regal
shine	scheinen, strahlen
ship	Schiff
shirt	Hemd

Vocabulary (Vokabeln)

shock	Schicksalsschlag, Schock
shocked at	schockiert über
shoe	Schuh
shoot	schießen
shop	Geschäft
shopping	Einkaufen
short	kurz
shot	Schuß, Spritze
should	soll
shoulder	Schulter
shout	schreien
shout at	anschreien
show	Kino, Theater, zeigen
shower	Dusche
shrink	einlaufen, schrumpfen
shut	schließen, zumachen
shy	schüchtern
sick	krank
sick of	satt haben, mehr als genug davon haben
side	Seite
sight	Anblick
sign	unterschreiben
silent	ruhig, stumm
silly	albern
similarly	ähnlich, gleichartig
simple	einfach
since	da, seit, seitdem
sincere	aufrichtig, echt
sing	singen
single	einzeln
sink	sinken
sister	Schwester
sit	sitzen
situation	Zustand
six	sechs
skiing	skilaufen
skirt	Rock
skunk	Stinktier
sky	Himmel
skyscraper	Hochhaus, Wolkenkratzer
slay	erschlagen, töten
sleep	schlafen
slice	Scheibe, Schnitte, Stück
slide	gleiten, schlittern

Vocabulary (Vokabeln)

sling	schleudern
slink	schleichen
slit	aufschneiden, schlitzen
slow	langsam
small	klein
smart	schlau
smell	duften, riechen
smile	lächeln
smoke	rauchen
snail	Schnecke
snatch	schnappen
snow	Schnee, schneien
so	also
soap	Seife
soccer	Fußballspiel
sock	Socke
so far	bis jetzt
soft	weich
soldier	Soldat
solve	lösen
some	etwas, irgendein
someone	jemand
something	etwas
sometimes	manchmal
somewhere	irgendwo
son	Sohn
song	Lied
soon	bald
as soon as	so bald wie
sooner than	früher als
soothe	beruhigen
sorry	Es tut mir leid.
sorry for	bedauere, traurig um
sort of	eine Art, etwas Derartiges, gewissermaßen
sound	fest, Geräusch, gesund, ganz, kräftig, tüchtig
sour	sauer
south	nach Süden
sow	säen
Spain	Spanien
spanking	Klaps, die Löffel kriegen
speak	reden, sprechen
speak to 'self	Selbstgespräche führen
specialize in	sich spezialisieren in
speed	beschleunigen, sich beeilen, schnell fahren

Vocabulary (Vokabeln)

spell	buchstabieren
spend	ausgeben, verbringen
spider	Spinne
spill	verschütten
spin	drehen, spinnen
spit	spucken
splash	bespritzen, planschen
splendid	herrlich
split	spalten, sich teilen
spoil	verderben, verwöhnen
spoon	Löffel
spread	ausbreiten, streichen
spring	Frühling, springen
square	viereckig
stable	Stall
stairs	Treppe
stamps	Briefmarken
stand	ausstehen, dulden, stehen
can't stand	kann nicht aushalten/ausstehen
start	anfangen
state	Aussagen, berichten, klarlegen, melden
station	Bahnhof
stay	bleiben
steady	beständig, standhaft, unerschütterlich
steal	stehlen
step	treten
steps	Treppen
stewardess	Stewardeß
stick	befestigen, heften, klebenbleiben, 'reinstecken, steckenbleiben
still	immer noch, noch, ruhig, still
sting	stechen
stink	stinken
stomach	Magen
stone	Stein
stop	aufhören
store	Geschäft
storm	Sturm
story	Geschichte
stove	Herd
straight	direkt, gerade, unmittelbar
strange	fremd
stranger	Fremder
strawberries	Erdbeeren

Vocabulary (Vokabeln)

street	Straße
strength	Kraft
stretch	strecken
stride	schreiten
strike	schlagen
string	aufreihen, spannen
strive	sich bemühen, streben
strong	stark
study	lernen, studieren
stumble	stolpern
stupid	doof, dumm
subclause	Nebensatz
submit 'self	sich unterwerfen
substitute	Ersatz, ersetzen
succeed in	gelingen
such	solch
suddenly	plötzlich
sugar	Zucker
suggest	andeuten, empfehlen, vorschlagen
suitable	passend
suitcase	Koffer
sum	Geldsumme, Gipfel, Menge
summer	Sommer
sums	Rechenaufgabe, Rechnen
sun	Sonne
sunbathe	sich sonnen
Sunday	Sonntag
sunny	sonnig
sunshine	Sonnenschein
supermarket	Supermarkt
supper	Abendbrot
support	Beistand, Unterstützung
support 'self	ernähren, unterstützen
suppose	annehmen, meinen, vermuten
be supposed to	soll, es wird erwartet
supreme	höchst, oberst
sure	sicher
surely	sicherlich, wahrhaftig, zweifellos
sure of	sich vergewissern
surprise	Überraschung
surprised at	sich wundern über
surrender 'self	sich ergeben
surrounded	eingekreist, umgeben

Vocabulary (Vokabeln)

survey	Marktstudie, schriftliche Überblick, schriftliche Übersicht, Umfrage
suspect of	im Verdacht haben wegen, Verdacht hegen
suspicious	mißtrauisch, verdächtig
swan	Schwan
swear	fluchen, schwören
sweep	kehren
sweet	süß
sweets	Süßigkeiten
swell	schwellen, zunehmen
swim	schwimmen
swing	schaukeln, schwingen
switch off	ausschalten, ausknipsen
table	Tisch
tablecloth	Tischdecke
tail	Schwanz
take	annehmen, machen, nehmen
take care of 'self	auf sich aufpassen/acht geben
take part in	teilnehmen
talent for	Begabung für
talk	reden, sprechen
talk about/of	sprechen von
talk to 'self	vor sich hinreden
tall	groß
task	Aufgabe
taste	Geschmack
taste for	Appetit auf, Neigung zu, Sinn für
tea	Tee
teach	lehren, unterrichten
teacher	Lehrer
tear	reißen, zerreißen
tease	necken
technically	technisch
technology	Technologie
teeth	Zähne
telephone	Telefon
television	Fernsehen
tell	befehlen, erklären, erzählen
temper	Wut, Zorn
tempt	verführen, in Versuchung führen
ten	zehn
tend	dazu neigen, gerichtet sein nach/auf
tense	Zeitform
terrible	schrecklich

Vocabulary (Vokabeln)

test	Klassenarbeit, Prüfung, Versuch
than	als
thank	sich bedanken
that is	das heißt
the	der, die, das
theatre	Bühne, Schauspielhaus, Theater
their	ihre
them	sie
then	dann
there	dort
therefore	deshalb
they	sie
thick	dick
thief	Dieb
thin	dünn
thing	Ding, Sache
think	denken, meinen
think of 'self	an sich denken
third	dritte
thirsty	durstig
this	dies
thoroughly	gründlich
those	jenes
though	obwohl
threaten	drohen
three	drei
thrill	Sensation, das Spannende, Spannung
thrilling	aufregend
through	durch
throw	werfen
thrust	stoßen
thumb	Daumen
Thursday	Donnerstag
thus	daher, folglich
ticket	Etikette, Fahrkarte, Fahrschein, Karte
tickle	kitzeln
tidy	aufgeräumt, ordentlich
tight	fest, stramm
till	bis
time	Mal, Zeit
tiny	klein, winzig
tired	erschöpft, müde
tired of	eine Sache satt haben
to	zu

Vocabulary (Vokabeln)

today	heute
toe	Zeh
tomorrow	morgen
tonight	heute abend
too	auch, außergewöhnlich, höchst, sehr
tooth	Zahn
toothache	Zahnschmerzen
totally	ganz, gesamt
touch	berühren
towel	Tuch
tower	Turm
town	Dorf
toy	Spielzeug
traffic	Verkehr
traffic light	Verkehrsampel
train	Zug
tram	Straßenbahn
travel	fahren, reisen
tread	treten
treat	behandeln
tree	Baum
triangular	dreieckig
trick	Scherz, Spaß
trip	Ausflug
trolley	Einkaufswagen, Karren
trouble	belästigen, beunruhigen, Mühe geben, stören
trouble 'self	sich die Mühe machen, sich sorgen
trousers	Hose
true, truly	aufrichtig, wahrhaftig, wirklich
trunk	Rüssel
trust	glauben, sich verlassen auf, vertrauen
truth	Wahrheit
try	versuchen mit, einen Versuch machen mit, vor Gericht bringen, durch Versuch feststellen
Tuesday	Dienstag
tune	Melodie
turkey	Puter, Truthahn
turn	drehen, an der Reihe sein, werden
TV	Fernsehen
twelve	zwölf
twenty	zwanzig
twice	zweimal
two	zwei
type	tippen

Vocabulary (Vokabeln)

typically	typisch
ugly	abstoßend, häßlich, widerwärtig
umbrella	Regenschirm
uncle	Onkel
under	unter
understand	begreifen, einsehen, verstehen
undertake	unternehmen, sich verpflichten
undoubtedly	unbestritten, zweifellos
unexpectedly	unerwartet
ungrateful	undankbar
unique	einmalig, einzigartig
universal	allumfassend, universal
university	Universität
unless	es sei denn, daß; vorausgesetzt
unlock	aufschließen, aufsperren, öffnen
unpleasant	unangenehm
until	bis
unusual	ungewöhnlich
unwilling	abgeneigt, nicht gewillt, ungern,
upset	aus der Fassung bringen, umwerfen, verwirren
upstairs	oben
up till now	bis jetzt
up to now	bis jetzt
urge	drängen, Drang, vorwärtstreiben, zwingen
us	uns
use	gebrauchen
used to	gewöhnt sein, pflegte zu tun
useful	nützlich
usually	gewöhnlich, normalerweise
utterly	völlig
vacation	Urlaub
value	hochachten, hochschätzen, Wert, Wert legen auf
very	rein, richtig, sehr, wirklich
visit	besuchen
visitor	Besucher
vocabulary	Vokabeln
voice	Stimme
volunteer	aus freien Stücken tun, sich freiwillig melden
vomit	ausbrechen, erbrechen, sich übergeben
vote	wählen
vow	feierlich versprechen, schwören
wager	Wette
wagging	wackeln mit, wedeln
wait	warten

Vocabulary (Vokabeln)

wait for	erwarten, warten auf
waiter	Kellner, Ober
waitress	Kellnerin
wake	aufwachen, aufwecken, erwachen
wake up	aufwachen, wecken
walk	laufen, Spaziergang
walking-stick	Spazierstock
wall	Wand
want	wollen
wardrobe	Garderobe, Kleiderschrank
warmer	wärmer
warn	ermahnen, warnen
warn against	warnen vor
warning	Mahnung, Warnung
wash	waschen
washing	Wäsche
waste	verschwenden
watch	beobachten, sehen, Uhr
water	begießen, Wasser
wave	winken
way	Art und Weise, Weg, weite Strecke
way of	Gelegenheit, Mittel, Verfahren, Weise . . . zu
we	wir
weak	schwach
wear	anhaben, tragen
weary of	satt, überdrüssig werden
weather	Wetter
weave	weben
Wednesday	Mittwoch
week	Woche
weekend	Wochenende
weekly	wöchentlich
weep	weinen
weight	Gewicht
welcome	keine Ursache, willkommen
well	gesund, gut, wohl
wet	naß
what	was
what about	Wie steht es mit?
wheelbarrow	Schubkarren
when	wann
whenever	jedesmal wenn, so oft als
where	wo
wherever	wo auch immer

Vocabulary (Vokabeln)

whether	ob
which	welche
while	während
whistle	pfeiffen
white	weiß
who	wer
whole, wholly	ausschließlich, durchaus, ganz, gänzlich, völlig
whom	wem, wen
whose	wessen
why	warum
wicked	böse, boshaft, schlecht
wide	weit
widow	Witwe
wife, wives	Ehefrau, -en
will	werden, wird
willing	bereitwillig, einverstanden, gewillt
willpower	Willenskraft
win	gewinnen
wind	aufdrehen, aufziehen, wickeln
window	Fenster
wine	Wein
wipe	wischen
wire	Draht
wise	weise
wish	Verlangen, Wunsch
with	mit
within	innerhalb
without	ohne
wolves	Wölfe
woman, women	Frau, -en
wonder	erstaunt sein, sich überlegen ob, sich wundern
wonderful	wunderbar
won't = will not	werden nicht
woods	Wald
word	Wort
work	Arbeit, arbeiten
workshop	Werkstätte
world	Welt
worms	Würmer
worry about	beunruhigen, sich Sorgen machen über
It is worth	sich lohnen, wert sein
would	würde
would rather	möchte lieber
would sooner	möchte eher

Vocabulary (Vokabeln)

wring	wringen
write	schreiben
wrong	falsch
year	Jahr
for years to come	auf Jahre hinaus
yearly	jährlich
yell	gellend schreien, laut anschreien
yellow	gelb
yes	ja
yesterday	gestern
yet	noch
yield	nachgeben, sich fügen
you	dich, dir, du, euch, Ihnen, ihr, Sie
young	jung
your	dein, euer, Ihrer
zoo	Tierpark, Zoo

Vokabeln (Vocabulary)

aber	but
Alkohol	alcohol
allein	alone
alles	all
alt	old
als	than
als ob	as if
Ameisen	ants
andere	other
anfangen	begin
anflehen	implore
Angst haben	to be afraid
ankommen	arrive
anrufen	phone
ansehen	look at
anziehen	get dressed, dress 'self
Arzt	doctor
aufbleiben	stay up
sich aufhalten	dwell on, stay
aufhören	discontinue, stop
aufräumen	clean up, tidy up
aufstehen	get up
Auto	car
backen	bake
Bahn	tram
bald	soon
Baustelle	building site
bedanken sich	decline, thank a person
bedienen sich	help 'self, serve
behaupten sich	assert 'self, keep one's ground, keep up
Bein	leg
bekommen	get, obtain, receive
benehmen sich	behave
Bescheid sagen	inform, instruct, tell
besser	better
besuchen	attend, visit
betrachten	consider, examine, look at, regard
betreten	enter
Bett	bed
Bild	picture
bis	until
bitten	ask
bleiben	remain, stay
Bleistift	pencil

Vokabeln (Vocabulary)

Blume	flower
brauchen nicht	don't have to, need not
Brief	letter
Brot	bread
Bruder	brother
Buch	book
da	as, because, there
dahin	there
Dame	lady
dann	then
daran	in it, to it
daß	that
dein	your
denken	imagine, think
deshalb	therefore
deutsch	German
Dienstag	Tuesday
doch	yes
dorthin	there
draußen	outside
drei	three
du	you
dürfen	be allowed to, be permitted to, may
eigentlich	really
einander	each other, one another
Einbrecher	burglar
Einkäufe machen	go shopping
Eis	ice, ice-cream
er	he
erwachsen werden	grow up
erwarten	expect
erwartet	expected
essen	eat
fahren	drive, go, travel
Fahrkarte	ticket
Fahrt	trip
falls	in case, if
fangen	catch, seize
fehlen	be absent, be missing
Feier	celebration
feiern	celebrate
Fenster	window
fernsehen	watch television
finden	find

Vokabeln (Vocabulary)

Fleisch	meat
fliegen	fly
Flugzeug	airplane, plane
folgen	follow
fragen	ask
Frau	woman
Freitag	Friday
fressen	eat
freuen sich	be happy, enjoy 'self, rejoice
Freund	friend
froh	glad, happy
früher	earlier, formerly
fühlen sich	feel
Füller	pen
fürchten	be afraid
zu Fuße gehen	walk
füttern	feed
gäbest	gave, would give
ganze	whole
geben	give
gebrochen	broken
Geburtstag	birthday
gefallen	like
gehen	go
Geld	money
genug	enough
gern	love to
Geschäft	shop
geschehen	happen
gestern	yesterday
ginge	went, would go
Haare	hair
haben	have
hätte	had, would have
Hand geben	shake hands
hassen	hate
Haus	house
nach hause	home
zu hause	at home
Hausaufgaben	homework
heiraten	get married
helfen	help
herumspringen	jump around
heute abend	this evening

Vokabeln (Vocabulary)

hier	here
hingehen	go there
Hochzeit	marriage, wedding
hören	hear, listen
hoffen	hope
hoffentlich	hopefully
holen	fetch, get
ich	I
ihm	him
ihn	him
immer	always
im Moment	at the moment
infolgedessen	therefore
Jahr	year
je	ever
jeden	each, every
jetzt	now
jung	young
Junge	boy
Kaffee	coffee
Kamera	camera
käme	came, would come
kämmen	comb
kann	can, is able to
Katze	cat
kaufen	buy
Kinder	children
Kino	cinema, movies, theater
Kirche	church
Klasse	class
Klassenarbeit	test
Klavier	piano
Kleid	dress
klein	little
König	king
können	can, could, be able to
kommen	come, get
krabbeln	crawl
krank	ill, sick
Krieg	war
Kuchen	cake
Küche	kitchen
küssen	kiss
lachen	laugh

Vokabeln (Vocabulary)

lange	long
lassen	leave, let
laufen	run, walk
laut	loud
leben	live
Lehrer	teacher
lernen	learn
lesen	read
letztes	last
Leute	people
lieb	dear, nice
lieben	love
Loch	hole
machen	do, take
Mädchen	girl
Mann	man
Maus	mouse
mein	my
meinen	believe, mean, think
mich	me
Milch	milk
mir	me
mitfahren	go along
mitgehen	accompany, go along
mitnehmen	take along
Mittwoch	Wednesday
möchten	want, would like
mögen	like, wish
Möglichkeit	possibility
im Moment	at the moment
Mond	moon
Montag	Monday
morgen	tomorrow
müde	tired
müssen	have to, must
mutig	brave, courageous
Mutter	mother
nach	after, following, to
nach Hause	home
Nacht	night
nächste	following, next
nähen	sew
nahe	close
Namen	name

Vokabeln (Vocabulary)

nehmen	take
nett	nice
neu	new
nicht	not
noch nicht	not yet
normal	normally
notwendig	necessary
nützlich	useful
ob	if, whether
oft	often
Oma	Grandmother
Onkel	uncle
Passagiere	passengers
Pferde	horses
Polizei	police
Prüfung	examination, test
putzen	clean, scour
Rasen	grass
rasieren sich	shave 'self
rauchen	smoke
rechte	right
Regen	rain
Regenschirm	umbrella
regnen	rain
reisen	travel
reiten	ride
reparieren	repair
Reste	left-overs, remains
rufen	call, shout
Satz	sentence
schämen sich	be ashamed
Scheibe	slice
es scheint	it seems
schlafen	sleep
schneiden	cut
schnell	quick
schon	already
schreiben	write
Schuh	shoe
Schule	school
Schulhof	playground
Schwein	pig
Schwester	sister
schwierig	difficult, hard

Vokabeln (Vocabulary)

schwimmen	swim
See	lake
sehen	see
sehr	very
sein	his
seit	for, since
selber	oneself
selbst	'self
Selbstgespräche führen	talk to 'self
setzen sich	seat 'self, sit down
sicher	safe
sie	her, she, them, they
singen	sing
sitzen	sit
sofort	at once, immediately
Sohn	son
sollen	ought to, should
Sonntag	Sunday
spät	late
Spiegelbild	mirror-image, see 'self in the mirror
spielen	play
sprechen	speak, talk
springen	jump
Stadt	city
ständig	constant, permanent
stattdessen	instead of that
stattfinden	take place
sterben	die
Straßenbahn	street car, tram
Stück	piece, slice
Stuhl	chair
Stunde	hour, lesson
suchen	look for, search, seek
täten	did, would do
Tag	day
tanzen	dance
Tisch	table
tot	dead
tragen	carry, take, wear
treffen	meet
trinken	drink
tun	do, make
überrascht	amazed, surprised

Vokabeln (Vocabulary)

übersetzen	translate
Uhr	o'clock
um	at
um zu	in order to
unglücklich	unhappy
unser	our
unterstützt	supported
Vater	father
Verben	verbs
verboten	forbidden, prohibited
vergessen	forget
verkaufen	sell
verlassen	abandon, leave, forsake
verletzt	hurt, injured
verlieben sich	fall in love
verlieren	lose
verpflichtet	commit, be s.o. duty
versprechen	promise
sich verständlich machen	make 'self understood
verstecken	hide
verstehen	understand
viel	many, much
vorbereitet	prepared
vorstellen sich	imagine, introduce 'self, suppose
vorziehen	choose, prefer
wählen	vote
wäre	were, would be
Wald	forest, woods
wann	when
warten	wait
warum	why
waschen	wash
Wasser	water
wegbringen	take away
weil	as, because
Wein	wine
weinen	cry
weit	far
wenn	when, whenever
werden	become, will
werfen	throw
Wetter	weather
wie	how

Vokabeln (Vocabulary)

wieder	again
wiederholen	repeat
wirklich	really
wissen	know, understand
Woche	week
wohl	indeed, probably, to be sure
wollen	want to
würde	would
Zahn	tooth
Zahnarzt	dentist
zeigen	show
ziehen	pull
Zimmer	room
zu	to, too
Zucker	sugar
zu Fuß gehen	walk
Zug	train
zu hause	at home
zusammennehmen	control 'self, gather, make an effort, pull 'self together, take care
zwei	two
zweimal	twice
zwingen	force